Future Search

FUTURE SEARCH

**AN ACTION GUIDE
TO FINDING COMMON GROUND
IN ORGANIZATIONS AND COMMUNITIES**

Marvin R. Weisbord and Sandra Janoff

Berrett-Koehler Publishers
San Francisco

Berrett-Koehler Publishers, Inc.
155 Montgomery St.
San Francisco, CA 94104-4109
Tel: (415) 288-0260 Fax: (415) 362-2512

Ordering Information
Individual sales. Berrett-Koehler publications are available through most bookstores. They can also be ordered direct from Berrett-Koehler at the address above.

Quantity sales. Special discounts are available on quantity purchases by corporations, associations, and others. For details, contact the "Special Sales Department" at the Berrett-Koehler address above.

Orders for college textbook/course adoption use. Please contact Berrett-Koehler Publishers at the address above.

Orders by U.S. trade bookstores and wholesalers. Please contact Publishers Group West, 4065 Hollis St., P.O. Box 8843, Emeryville, CA 94662; Tel: (510) 658-3453; 1-800-788-3123; Fax: (510) 658-1834.

Printed in the United States of America

 Printed on acid-free and recycled paper that is composed of 85% recovered fiber, including 15% post consumer waste.

Library of Congress Cataloging-in-Publication Data

Weisbord, Marvin Ross.
 Future search : finding common ground for action in organizations and communities / by Marvin R. Weisbord & Sandra Janoff. — 1st ed.
 p. cm.
 Includes bibliographical references and index.
 ISBN 1–881052–12–5 (alk. paper)
 1. Planning—Methodology. 2. Social action—Planning—Methodology 3. Active learning—Planning. 4. Congresses and conventions—Planning. I. Janoff, Sandra. II. Title.
HD30.28.W378 1995
302.3'5—dc20 95–14073
 CIP

First Edition
 99 98 97 96 95 10 9 8 7 6 5 4 3 2 1

Cover Design by Barbara Gelfand and Mary Sanichas
Photos by Allan Kobernick
Book Design by Pacific West Publishing Service

Contents

Section Two: DOING

Section Three: RESOURCES

Dedication

To the memory of Eric Trist, our friend and mentor,
and to SearchNet members everywhere
who carry on.

Preface

This is a guide for people seeking common ground for action in organizations and communities. A future search is a large group planning meeting that brings a "whole system" into the room to work on a task-focused agenda. The meeting is based on a simple notion: if we want dramatic new action plans, we need to use structures and processes congruent with our aspirations. Such aspirations – sometimes labeled "cultural transformation" or "paradigm shift" – seem abstract, elusive, and hard to initiate. They can, however, be experienced and used to practical advantage by those willing to work under a set of conditions that we will describe in this book.

In a future search, people have a chance to take ownership of their past, present, and future, confirm their mutual values, and commit to action plans grounded in reality. Everybody is invited to share leadership and participate as peers. Participants often set in motion many new kinds of working relationships and projects. Thus this meeting provides a glimpse of a world more realistic and attainable than many people believe is possible.

To experience that, however, requires a leap into uncharted territory that not everyone is ready to take. For example, we often include total strangers or folks with a history of conflict. We open the door to people's diverse

agendas. We generate confusing and contradictory information. We do not strive to reduce complexity to a few manageable issues, to resolve disagreements, or to solve long-standing problems. Nor do we give people a management model for organizing their diverse perceptions.

Instead, we set up a series of open dialogues. We encourage listening and understanding what others are saying. We work toward the discovery and use of common agendas and shared ideals rather than the replay of old patterns of interaction. People discover what they are ready, willing, and able to do now. Under these conditions many folks make choices previously unavailable.

Examples number in the hundreds. A Massachusetts future search conference, for example, shook loose in a few weeks a bill critical to small manufacturers that had been bottled up for years in the state legislature. Citizens of Santa Cruz County, California, got contentious housing issues out of a frustrated committee and into a forum of ongoing action projects among developers, funders, social activists, business-people, educators, religious groups, migrant workers, and officials. A Texas firm, Whole Foods Market, used a future search to plan its national expansion and, after many mergers, repeated the process five years later to unify its diverse corporate cultures.

Learning to Find Common Ground

There are many advantages to having a diverse group plan and act together on a common future. Not the least is a shared picture of reality that no participants had when they came through the door. Freed from problem solving and conflict managing, people discover a new freedom to make things happen. Because the right people are in the room, we see faster follow-through. A great many people experience the power of voluntary commitments made on common ground.

This book describes principles and tools that you can use to create a context for rapid, innovative planning. In particu-

lar, we emphasize the dynamics that we believe help people move from feelings of impotence and frustration toward greater hope, reality, mutual support, creative ideas, and shared responsibility. In this sense future search serves as a metaphor for managing amid relentless uncertainty. It provides a process with many remarkable possibilities based on the latent values, aspirations, and skills that participants already have.

To engage in a series of dialogues embracing both hope and despair is to discover that we have real *choices*. We can throw up our hands and run or we can choose the path of social, technological, and economic innovation. Paradoxically, many task-focused meetings aim at eliminating or avoiding anxiety, often through detailed data analysis. In a future search, anxiety becomes an energy source. We treat it as a fact of life, not as a problem solvable with more data. Above all we do not "fast-forward" through the hard parts.

Future search combines task and process in such a way as to open up real choices of consequence. We believe that staying with "the mess," and suspending decisions, conflicts, and problem solving until we have a shared fix on what's doable accounts for the high degree of implementation that typically follows a future search. Indeed, nearly everyone finds their outlook changing as they carry out the conference task. Task-oriented people, suspending the drive to act *now*, experience a radical new way of relating to the world and to each other. Process-oriented folks, acting on common ground after only a few hours of discussion (leaving some deep issues unexplored), also are taking an unfamiliar path. Engaging successfully in these meetings with so many different people and agendas constitutes change of a high order for a large cross-section of our society.

Who Can Benefit From Future Search?

We have written our book with certain readers in mind. If you are responsible for the future of your organization or community, you will find here a structure and process that

have helped many others do good planning in problematic situations. You will learn the origins and dynamics of the meeting, the careful planning and facilitating required, and the potential for working with issues that have no easy answers. If you own or manage a business, you will learn how to speed up action and commitment in your firm.

If you are a veteran large group facilitator, you can use this book to compare our experiences with yours and to broaden your action repertoire. If you are new to large group facilitation, you can use it as a reference for planning your learning needs (perhaps with a mentor or in a public workshop). And facilitators and consultants, whatever their experience, may find here as well the rationale, and therefore the courage, to say "no" to requests for service that they believe will fall short of their own and their clients' expectations.

Finally, if you are on a future search steering committee, you will discover why the success of your conference depends mainly on your decisions about who, what, when, and where. All readers will get an inside view of the nuts, bolts, and dynamic issues they can expect to encounter, with many concrete examples. In particular, we will show you that success in a future search is not in the techniques but in the principles and values that govern its management. Still, you need techniques to begin with. This book displays ours and tells how we learned them.

Taking Responsibility for Our Future

Why future search? As a society we have painted ourselves into a technological corner. We have more ways to do things than ever before. Yet a lot of what matters to us is not getting done, despite the large sums we spend on public and corporate business. Our computers get faster every year. Yet our psyches are not swift enough to keep up with them. Our information on a vast array of human concerns far exceeds our ability to interpret or act on it. The more we learn, the more helpless we feel. Cars get faster and we sit in traffic jams. We spend a fortune on medical care, but not everybody

has coverage and those who do may lose it when they need it most. Many of us fill jobs where we can't use the brains we were born with, or live in communities where we feel helpless to influence public policy. We experience high walls between haves and have nots, experts and amateurs, leaders and followers. As a society we suffer isolation, cynicism, and a sense that the world is spinning out of control.

In future search meetings people have a chance to take down the walls and assume more control of their future. Many participants welcome the chance to take responsibility for themselves and to learn and work with people from other walks of life. People are always more secure knowing first hand where others stand, and may begin in this setting to accept differences – in background, viewpoints, and values – as realities to be lived with, not problems to be solved. Many people start to revise their stereotypes as they embrace new working coalitions. They discover resources in themselves and others that they didn't know were there. Surprising projects become possible. Future search is a simple meeting structure with profound implications for organizations and communities everywhere.

Origins of This Book

This book started as a half dozen flip charts in an experimental workshop. In 1991, Gil Levin, director of the Cape Cod Institute of the Albert Einstein College of Medicine, offered us a chance to present our methods. His offer raised several dilemmas. First, we knew how to organize future searches, but had never run a future search seminar. We had doubts that our method was teachable. Believing in experience-based learning, we had a hard time imagining how to communicate this process in lectures and discussions. We didn't like the apparent contradiction that our workshop participants would be united only by a desire to learn a method designed for groups with common stakes in acting together. They could experience the techniques but not the dynamics that grip people as they work toward joint action.

More, we were not satisfied with our design, having changed it repeatedly over the years. We almost said, "no."

On the other hand...we knew that future search processes were *learnable*. Many people had devised conferences after reading a description in Chapter 14 of *Productive Workplaces* (Weisbord, 1987). A spontaneous outpouring of successful examples led to *Discovering Common Ground* (Weisbord et al, 1992), a book of cases, theory, and underlying principles from around the world. Comparing notes with many colleagues, we began to understand our structure and processes in a deeper way. We realized there were many subtleties to the apparently simple techniques. We also concluded we were evolving our own model, reflecting not only our sources but our particular experience, gained over many years, with personal, group and large system change processes.

We were curious to know how far we could go in encouraging others to explore this path. We decided to use the Cape Cod seminar to find out if folks could grasp future search principles short of an actual conference. Before we knew it, nearly 100 people signed up, an astonishing ground swell of interest in a concept we thought had a very selective fan club. Afterwards, a number of people found the courage to run conferences. More, we learned enough to want to do it again – though with smaller groups!

SearchNet Expands the Possibilities

About the same time, some Philadelphia Region Organization Development Network members, led by Marilyn Sifford, asked if we would help them learn future search methods. Together we devised a self-managed internship project, offering pro bono conferences to local non-profit agencies. This gave us a chance to involve conference sponsors in the training, greatly increasing the reality for all of us. Some 30 conferences resulted, and we began hearing from folks in other cities wanting to work pro bono in their communities as a way to learn this process. In 1992 we founded SearchNet, a non-profit program aimed at learning,

service, and colleagueship. Fortunately, we were able to affiliate with Resources for Human Development, Inc., a Philadelphia-based umbrella for more than 100 innovative community programs – homeless shelters, residential drug treatment facilities, art outreach, job training, support groups, child care, affordable housing, and other social action projects.

In little more than a year 300+ folks from North America and abroad had joined us in SearchNet. Our learning laboratory had become a lightning rod for many emotionally-charged currents in our society. This energy was coming from people fed up with fruitless meetings and methods that promised much and delivered little. Many people were using future search to plan and implement projects they had not been able to do before. Our experimental future search process gave us more hope than any of us expected.

Now hundreds of folks are running future search meetings – in schools, hospitals, churches, business firms, and communities. Thousands of people have become involved. That's not many compared to the need, but it's a good start. SearchNet affiliates exist in several cities across North America, and associates in many parts of the world want to set up service networks. This base has stimulated a demand for more access to shared learning. Our book is one response.

Enabling Constructive Action

We see future search as a building block of theory and practice for a house that will never be finished. This book is neither the first word nor the last. We think of it as a progress report from our learning laboratory. The roller-coaster ride inherent in a successful future search is inevitable, but we believe there are many ways to navigate the twists and turns. Words change, contexts shift, conceptual schemes come and go, but the human business of muddling through life's ups and downs together strikes us as a universal process. We believe these meetings are good for us and good for society. We hope this work enables thousands of constructive action projects in organizations and communities everywhere.

Acknowledgments

This book reflects 25 years of work and countless conferences by us and many colleagues. We acknowledge all the folks with whom we have had phone calls, meetings, discussions, workshops, and planning sessions. In particular, we have been fortunate to be a part of a Philadelphia Region OD Network future search community service project, a major stimulus for this book. Planning meetings and discussions with Nancy Aronson, Beverly Arsht, Carole Cohn, Ralph Coplemen, Marti Kaplan, Ferne Kuhn, Marilyn Sifford, John VanDeusen, and Michele Woods have been specially helpful.

SearchNet, an essential context for our work, owes its existence to the enthusiastic support of Robert Fishman and Dyann Mowatt of Resources for Human Development, Inc., and its continuance to the energy of Maria Mitros, our program administrator. We also acknowledge the many SearchNet members named in the text who have contributed their experience to cases and examples we cite. We have learned from Steve Burgess' explorations in group creativity, and from regular dialogues with Bill Schmidt in California, John Evans and Tony Richardson in Australia, and Chris Schoch in France.

Billie Alban, Don Benson, Randy Evans, David Klein, Steve McIntosh, Steve McMillan, Gil Steil, and Robert Tannenbaum made helpful suggestions for revising the manuscript.

We thank the dozens of conference sponsors who went out on a limb to use this methodology and enlarged our learning laboratory. Thanks also to Steve Piersanti for pushing us to write a more complete account than we imagined we could, to Alan Trist for his respectful editing, book design, and collaboration, reflecting a deep commitment to this work, and to Allan Kobernick for his dynamic color images and design help. Our spouses, Dorothy B. Weisbord and Allan Kobernick, our children and their families all have been unfailingly supportive of our work.

Marvin Weisbord and Sandra Janoff
Philadelphia, Pennsylvania
February, 1995

Future Search

"A man was walking on the beach and saw a small boy throwing starfish into the ocean. There were millions of them. 'What difference, young man,' he asked, 'can that possibly make, throwing starfish one at a time?' The boy just picked up another starfish. 'It's gonna make a big difference to this one,' he said."

– Participant, Santa Cruz Housing Conference

common
into
ons."

er Lasch

Productive Work-
parked to it that we
ke "strategic futures
e to the concept led to
ord et al, 1992), a work
practices for value-based
presented a variety of high
participation models and cases, most based on the Emery/
Trist Search Conference, including early experiments with
future search.

In this book we focus on our evolving future search
model. Here we go deeply into our sources and rationale, our
experiments with tasks and techniques, and examples of how
we and many colleagues have employed this model and its
variations. We also provide a philosophical rationale for our
design and facilitation practices.

Productive Workplaces showed how managing has evolved
from experts solving problems for people toward everybody,
experts included, improving whole systems.

In this book we focus more narrowly and deeply on processes that enable everybody to take more responsibility for themselves *and* for the whole – whether a community, network, or organization. Obviously, "everybody" is a metaphor. In practice we get as varied a group as we can, consistent with our purposes. We see future search as a learning laboratory for "getting everybody improving whole systems." It is not the complete answer to anything. Yet the dynamics apply to many kinds of meetings and change strategies. To experience this method in a single meeting is to open many new doors. Our society has hardly begun to explore what we can do with diverse parties working on the same task.

What Makes Future Search Conferences Different?

Future search conferences enable organizations and communities to learn more about themselves from every angle. Bringing the "whole system" into the room makes feasible a shared encounter with aspects of reality we normally avoid – chaos, complexity, uncertainty. The key word is "shared." When we explore common ground with others, we release creative energy leading to projects none of us can do alone. People simultaneously discover mutual values, innovative ideas, commitment, and support. Rarely in daily life do people encounter these key conditions for action all at once.

Our method is time efficient. We don't have to teach people anything for them to participate. They need not master our conceptual scheme to do good planning. They need only show up and use the skills, experience, and motivation they already have. That makes a lot of sense when you can schedule only four or five half-days together. We are seeking what people already want to do and never dreamed they could. Future search is not a substitute for rational planning procedures. Rather we provide an umbrella for building commitment. Our forum allows people to work far enough through the dynamic issues that stand in the way of implementing anything – dreams and schemes, systems and projects, visions and values.

Three Generic Uses

The uses of future search fall into three broad categories.

One, future search processes lead stakeholders to create a shared future vision for their organization or community. This simplicity of purpose ensures that many issues will be planned for in relation to each other. Santa Cruz County, CA, for example, came to a host of agreements on transportation, multi-cultural cooperation, employment, and education, although their conference topic started with affordable housing.

Two, future search meetings enable all stakeholders to discover shared intentions and take responsibility for their own plans. For

example, Haworth Incorporated's customers, suppliers, and employees fixed major waste disposal problems out of a shared appreciation of environmental concerns in a conference built around quality.

Three, these events can help people implement a shared vision that already exists. In Kansas City, MO, 130 people from every sector created an implementation strategy for city-wide goals that grew from two years of work by thousands of citizens. People came to the conference committed to their vision and left with aligned strategies for getting there.

A Short Overview

Our future search also has certain limits – of task focus and sequence, group size and composition, and length. Over several years we have sought to integrate these elements so that ordinary people can do extraordinary work. Our conference design depends on a set of mutually-reinforcing practices or "conditions for success." The list captures our optimal criteria for realizing the full potential of this event.

CONDITIONS FOR SUCCESS

- "Whole system" in the room

- Global context, local action

- Common ground and future focus,

 not problems and conflicts

- Self-managed small groups

- Full attendance

- Healthy meeting conditions

- 3 day event (i.e. "sleep twice")

- Public responsibility for follow-up

Structure

Our conferences typically involve 60 to 70 people. Our purpose is always joint action toward a desired future for a community, organization, or issue. We do five simple tasks:

- Review the Past
- Explore the Present
- Create Ideal Future Scenarios
- Identify Common Ground
- Make Action Plans

Work on the past and future is always done by mixed groups that are a cross-section of the whole. Work in the present is done by "stakeholder" groups whose members have some shared perspective on the task. Action planning employs both stakeholder and self-selected groups. Every task concludes with a whole group dialogue.

Riding the Roller-Coaster

The task sequence and group composition set up powerful dynamics that can lead to constructive outcomes. Uncertainty, frustration, and confusion are necessary by-products. So are fun, energy, and achievement. We experience the conference's peaks and valleys as an emotional roller-coaster ride, swooping down into the morass of global trends at one moment, soaring to idealistic heights at another. Future search sets up a counterpoint between hope and despair. We believe good contact with our ups and downs leads to realistic choices.

We always have people with differing assumptions and ways of learning present at the conference. Some folks, for example, need facts first, others tune in on feelings. We don't know how to design a planning meeting exclusively for the needs of one group or the other. Fortunately, the solution is simpler than you might think. In a future search we live with the inevitability of differences, the recognition that no meet-

ing design can reconcile them – and the belief that people are capable of new action plans without "more data" or "more dialogue" – in a very short time, if they agree to keep working together.

They can do that in a future search because no training, inputs, data collection, or diagnoses are required. In short, people face each other rather than a set of concepts, expert advice, or assumptions about what they lack and what they ought to do. The method involves comparing notes and listening. People discover hidden capacities through a cold plunge into self-generated reality, including ideals and the mish-mash of assumptions, misinformation, stereotypes, and judgments rattling around in all of us. Amazingly, it is *not* necessary to straighten all this out to succeed. What we aspire to in a future search is to acknowledge what we discover as an inescapable part of our shared world, whether we like it or not. In short, we look for buried potential that already exists without having to remedy perceived deficiencies.

*"This process
makes it really
clear that we see
everybody in the
community as an
asset. Most of
all, we all have a
personal respon-
sibility to partici-
pate in our
society to make
it better."*

Moving Toward Implementation

Future search conferences often enable people to experience and accept polarities. They help participants bridge barriers of culture, class, age, gender, ethnicity, power, status, and hierarchy *by working as peers on tasks of mutual concern.* The future search process interrupts the tendency to repeat old patterns – railroading, fighting, running away, complaining, blaming, or waiting for others to fix things. And it gives people a chance to express their highest ideals. Instead of trying to change the world or each other, we change the conditions under which people interact. That much we can control and it leads to surprising outcomes.

The single most worrisome aspect of planning is implementation. No process, however comprehensive, guarantees action. Still, we have seen more plans implemented from future searches than any method either of us has used in 25 years. The cases in Chapter 2 provide good examples. People act quite apart from whether they had a good time, liked the

facilitators, collected handouts, resolved their differences, or felt finished. Nor is success a function of how complete an action planning format we use. Action requires people who understand and believe in their shared goals and trust each other enough to join in new steps. It also requires committing resources – of time and energy, and sometimes money. We think future search fosters this understanding, belief, and commitment.

How Future Search Pushes the Boundaries of OD

We see future search extending traditional organization development (OD) meetings in a new direction. First off, OD was conceived not as a single meeting but rather a strategy for large-scale cultural and/or systemic change. Future search describes a process for one meeting lasting fewer than three days with the potential for ongoing action. Second, where OD depended on many people accepting the "need for change," future search depends on 60 – 70 people accepting an invitation to spend a few days together.

Thirdly, organization development, at least until recently, was based on diagnosing gaps between what is and what ought to be. Consultants supplied a diagnostic framework, applied interviews or surveys, and used the information to create dissonance between what people did and what they said. This was intended to "unfreeze" a system, leading people to want to reorder their relationships and capabilities. Consultants also accepted responsibility for prescribing action steps to close the gaps. These actions might include team-building, leadership, interpersonal and/or group skills training, or problem-solving task forces. Nearly always the action steps involved training, on the theory that people did not know how to do what they said they wanted to do.

To run a future search, we need no diagnosis of what ails people or categories for labeling participants (e.g., "cooperative," "resistant," etc.). Nor do we require strategies for fixing this or that situation. We have no preconceived issues to

*Margin quotes come from audio transcripts of conferences with Resources for Human Development, Whole Foods Market, Santa Cruz County (CA), Quaker Oats (Topeka, KS), and a Silicon Valley (CA) manufacturing initiative.

explore other than the past, present, and future as viewed by participants. In truth, we can't imagine a set of concepts for organizing data or action plans that would meet the needs of diverse future search groups.

We don't work to improve relationships among people or functions. Rather we set up conditions under which people can choose new ways of relating. We don't abstract out social issues (e.g., diversity, trust, communications, collaboration, etc.) from economic and technical issues. We are unlikely to run a conference on "the future of diversity in X." Rather, we'd propose that diverse people explore together how they want to live and work as part of X. Whatever peoples' skills, education, or experience, they already have what they need to engage in this process.

Experiencing "Current Reality"

"One wonderful element of future search is that it gives individuals a chance to take responsibility. That's an enormous difference from a task force list of recommendations for someone else to take care of."

As facilitators of a future search, we don't judge information as good or bad, complete or sketchy, useful or futile, appropriate or redundant. Whatever people do or say – their words, their behavior, their wishes, and their reactions – belongs to them. Whatever happens is an expression of the stakeholders, for better or worse. We don't expect dramatic individual change, only a change in the action potential among individuals, based on discovering new alignments. For example, people will not suddenly give up authority/dependency needs because they spent a few days as peers. But they may learn more about their ability to work together with more shared authority.

So we are interested that participants experience what already exists – as fully, deeply, and humanly as possible in the time available. That includes the past, which is always present, feelings and behavior in the present, and future aspirations, which also exist only in the present. Then people are more likely to make rational choices about what they want to do. We believe that acknowledging all of the above to each other *before* figuring out what to do is a good way to stay sane in a world that is changing unceasingly whether we like it or not.

Ours is an encounter with the whole – self, community, world. But we do not provide an expert systems analysis for people to consider. Rather, we set up a situation that involves the whole person on many levels. We ask people to share the work, move around, make their wishes visible, live with uncertainty. In a future search people experience a different version of "reality" than the one they are used to. They talk over issues they have not raised before with people they have never met. Many will take responsibility for matters previously avoided or ignored. They dramatize ideal futures as if they have actually happened, thus anchoring them in first-hand experience. They identify what they *really* want. It is common for people to voluntarily commit to actions made possible only because of the other people in the room. We have sought a design that moves us towards *all* of the above, because we believe *all* of the above adds up to sustained action.

Our procedures evolved while working mainly with folks who can read and write. However, the underlying principles do not depend on literacy. We believe this work could be done entirely with spoken and/or symbolic communication. The results have been repeated in many cultures and in culturally diverse groups. Indeed, *any* techniques that help people explore their whole system, experience their common stakes, share their ideals, internalize the experience, and take responsibility for what happens are worth applying.

We believe conferences designed on principles we have adopted lead to (1) participants taking personal responsibility, (2) fast implementation of action plans, and (3) lasting relationships across key boundaries. For now, this is a tantalizing hypothesis – an unproved theory. The only way to test it is to find out what participants do afterwards that they couldn't do before. Our evidence is largely anecdotal. Still, good stories abound, enough to keep us going on this path. To evaluate our experiments, see if you can recreate our key conditions and track what happens over time.

A Learning Laboratory

Having said all that, we see future search as a learning laboratory. We set the wheels in motion for a variety of discoveries, starting with whether we can raise the right crowd. We never know in advance what people are ready, willing, and able to do. We never know what dynamics are likely to be central to a given group, or what issues they will emphasize when they talk about world trends. We still don't know all the conditions under which people will take responsibility for their own planning. We know at least one under which they won't: when a meeting is set up to replay old scripts.

A future search deliberately offers participants a new, unfamiliar, but learnable, way of working. Not everybody takes full advantage of the mode; not everybody believes in it; not everybody can tolerate doing so much so fast, or, as some see it, doing nothing at length. And yet. . . and yet, we know we are on to something. And so are the hundreds of others experimenting with this mode.

*"This is a great exercise in democracy...
to let people come together to talk about what's troubling them and their community, and they can plan for change."*

Design Limits – In Systems, In Us

Within our design limits there's a lot we can do. But our meeting design is not a panacea. We can't compensate, for example, for lack of purpose, leadership, broad stakeholder involvement, or courage. We can't affect people who don't attend nor can we expect others to take responsibility for plans made without them. Moreover, ours is not a method for negotiating compromises on intractable differences. Nor for working through all the assumptions that underlie our conflicts. We are actualizing what is waiting to happen, what people can do readily in the short time available.

Future search works on quite different principles from most meetings. We're not surprised when potential sponsors and consultants worry about the structure and process. We all fear losing control, opening up issues we'd rather not air, or hearing demands we can't meet. Future search takes us very quickly into uncharted territory. We cannot know what

will happen until we get there. Rarely have we led a conference where, at some moment, we did not feel anxiety. There is nothing to do about this feeling except to recognize it as an old friend. The situation will change soon enough. Our "solution" is to encourage people to say what needs to be said and to keep working on the task. We have great confidence that people will do what's appropriate.

We believe the key principles of future search are widely applicable to the day-to-day management of both organizations and communities. To use them, though, we can't just work on systems "out there." We also need to work on ourselves. In particular, we have to learn to let go of the need to fix other people. We hear many questions that start, "Yes, but how do you get *them* to..." followed by "show up," "stay the whole time," "really listen to each other," "resist problem-solving," "test each other's assumptions," "not talk too much," "say what they really think in front of so-and-so," "make practical plans," "really understand systems," or "implement A, B, or C?"

Our answer is, "We can't." Even if we could, we wouldn't. The spirit of future search is self-management and discovery. We expect participants to share leadership and organize their own work. We tell people everything we know about success. We show up only when we think we will succeed. And we trust people to do whatever is in their own best interest. If folks will come to a future search, stay the whole time, and say what they wish, we ask no more.

Related Processes

Many conference processes overlap ours. The best known is the Search Conference pioneered by Eric Trist and Fred Emery (Weisbord et al, 1992) and developed further by Fred and Merrelyn Emery (1993). Our method owes a great deal to their work and differs from it in several respects – for example, our emphasis on the "whole system" in the room, the nature and sequence of small group tasks, and in our evoking personal experiences and creative future scenarios as a back-

drop for action. Another related process is the Dialogue Group of the late physicist David Bohm, developed further by William Isaacs and his colleagues at Massachusetts Institute of Technology. We share with this model the norm that all issues are valid and that all views be heard. Unlike dialogue groups, future searches are task-focused, actively managed, structured, and time-bound toward action on the future.

Open Space Technology, invented by Harrison Owen (1992) is also related. In Open Space people select their agendas and groups, while in a future search predetermined groups work the same tasks toward a common future. Both models invite participants to manage their own small group tasks and both build a strong communal spirit. A fourth related process is the participative strategic planning conferences of Kathleen Dannemiller and Robert Jacobs (1993). We share with this model a common ancestor in the large-group meetings of Ronald Lippitt and Eva Schindler-Rainman (1980). In the Dannemiller/Jacobs conferences leaders take a central role in setting the context, giving information on future directions, and fielding questions. In a future search, leaders, experts, and special interests participate in all tasks along with everybody else. Also, the Dannemiller/Jacobs and Owen conferences can accommodate hundreds of people at once in contrast to our preferred 64 and the Emerys' 32.

We continue to learn from, encourage, and support all these processes. Their similarities and differences seem minor to us compared to the fact that so many folks are exploring methods for helping people experience wholeness in a time of unprecedented complexity, bewilderment, and change. We believe that no combination of theories or techniques embraces the whole of reality. For us, the concept of "best model" is an anachronism. We think the metaphor for these methods is a kaleidoscope. We are all working with the same bits of colored glass, evoking new patterns as we gain experience. We believe that the "best model" for you is one that squares with your goals, values, and capabilities. Indeed, you can use no other.

Several people are merging large-group events into new change strategies, based in part on future search. Examples include Dick and Emily Axelrod's "Conference Model" for work design, and a similar strategy devised by Margaret Wheatley and Myron Kellner-Rogers. Ralph Copleman has experimented with sequencing future search and Open Space methods. Several folks are experimenting with multiple conferences in parallel and in series. The strategic and logistical questions raised by such conferences, however, are outside the scope of this book. We urge the reader to learn how to run single events with manageable-size groups before getting into multiple anythings. We have a relatively narrow agenda here – how to plan and facilitate one 16+ hour event spread across three days. We see this as a basic building block of social and personal change.

How the Book Is Organized

Section 1: "Learning" – provides a design overview (Chapter 1) and case examples (Chapter 2). We discuss conditions for success (Chapter 3). Chapters 4 and 5 deal with issues of translating theory into practice and the evolution of our design.

Section 2: "Doing" – goes into three equally important activities: finding conference sponsors (Chapter 6), planning conferences (Chapters 7 and 8), facilitating (Chapter 9), and what folks do to keep action plans alive (Chapter 10).

Section 3: "Resources" – Appendices A through D include logistics – room set-up and materials – a participant workbook, our design, and a sample invitation. We also provide practical guidelines on finding and setting up conference rooms.

CHAPTER 1

The Future Search Meeting Design

An Overview of Tasks and Dynamics

> "When you listen to somebody else,
> whether you like it or not, what they say
> becomes a part of you...the common pool is
> created, where people begin suspending
> their own opinions and listening to other
> peoples'....At some point people begin
> recognizing that this common pool is more
> important than their separate pools."
>
> – David Bohm

HERE WE WALK YOU THROUGH a future search conference, showing tasks and time-frames, what the output is, which groups do what, and the dynamic issues that emerge at each stage. The task sequence and timing are deliberate. We proceed from reviewing the past and owning the present to describing a common future and action plans. We have found that this sequence can produce superior planning when the key conditions are observed. (For an example of the work plan we actually use in running a conference, see Appendix C.)

By "future search" we mean our generic design, based on five tasks of two to four hours each, spread over three days. We do not mean conference events that use the same language or worksheets and bypass the conditions for success (see Chapter 3).

```
┌─────────────────────────────────────────────┐
│        TYPICAL FUTURE SEARCH AGENDA          │
│   Day 1, Afternoon                           │
│      • Focus on the Past                     │
│      • Focus on Present, External Trends     │
│   Day 2, Morning                             │
│      • continued – Trends                    │
│      • Focus on Present, Owning our Actions  │
│   Day 2, Afternoon                           │
│      • Ideal Future Scenarios                │
│      • Identify Common Ground                │
│   Day 3, Morning                             │
│      • continued – Confirm Common Ground     │
│      • Action Planning                       │
└─────────────────────────────────────────────┘
```

"By constructing a vertical slice of the community, we put people on a level playing field where each one had a chance to be a leader. The future search process really brought out those leadership skills."

Let us walk you through a typical session, covered in detail in Chapter 5.

Day 1 – Afternoon

The conference opens between noon and 5 pm on Day 1. The first day requires about 4 1/2 hours. People sit in mixed groups, each a cross-section of the whole conference, doing tasks that establish common ground.

The first task, focus on the past, takes about 2 1/2 hours. There are long strips of butcher paper on the walls, with titles: "Personal," "Global," and "X" (i.e., community, organization, issue), and dates every 5 or 10 years. People note milestones they have experienced over XX years on worksheets and transfer their notes to the long strips on the wall. Then, in small groups they talk over the trends and patterns that they see. They prepare public summaries of stories derived from everybody's experiences, and the whole conference discusses what they have learned.

This task gets every person in the room writing on flip charts within the first 45 minutes, showing that they all have valid information and experience. Moving around is encour-

aged. All items remain on the walls to the end of the confer-
ence and belong to everyone. The task builds community
very quickly as people experience the world through each
other's eyes.

We then move on to a focus on the present. Before the day
ends, the whole group reviews external trends that are shap-
ing our lives and institutions now. We put the group's
perceptions of world trends into a "mind map." Everybody
gets to hear each person's observations and examples of
trends they consider important. "My facts" and "your facts"
become "our facts." (See Chapter 5 for details on mind
mapping.)

This can be a mind-boggling experience. Some feel a
strong urge to run away. Instead, people confront the com-
plexity, approaching the map and affixing colored dots to
trends they consider important. Everybody touches the map.

Thus the stage is set for discussing and accepting responsibility for action. The point of the exercise is *not* to set priorities. Rather it's a step toward dialogue and manageability. The session ends here to provide the benefits of "soak time" over night.

Day 2 – Morning

In the morning we continue our focus on the present, confirming with the whole group the key trends noted the day before. We now reorganize into "stakeholder groups," people with a shared relationship to the overall conference task. These groups identify trends important to them, and report to the whole what they are doing and what they want to do in the future about these trends. This is often a turning point in the conference. Groups experience each other owning up and taking responsibility. People often comment on this in the large group discussion.

Next, we revisit the present. Each stakeholder group makes lists of "prouds" and "sorries" about what they are doing in relationship to "X." Each group's lists are viewed as "current reality," not as problems to be solved. Lists are reported and discussed in the large group. The purpose is ownership, not finger-pointing. We often hear some variation on the Pogo phenomenon, "We have met the enemy and he is us!"

Day 2 – Afternoon

Now we are ready to focus on the future. People return to mixed groups to prepare ideal future scenarios. They have about 2 ½ hours, including lunch. They are asked to put themselves 10 to 20 years in the future and present their scenario concretely as if it were happening now. They tell how they overcame barriers along the way.

By imagining and then acting out ideal futures, people anchor them in their brains, bodies, and psyches – tapping unconscious aspirations, making visible what they *really* want. People present their futures in whatever way they wish. We have seen scenarios that have been playful, funny,

A Note to Readers Who Have Seen
Earlier Versions of this Design

Like all practitioners working with living ideas, we continue to experiment with techniques. Some aspects of this outline will be new to future search workshop participants prior to May 1994. They reflect changes in both wording and substance. For example:

Review of the Past: We use time lines drawn on strips of butcher paper rather than vertical flip charts.

Focus on the Future: We call our future scenarios ideal futures because we want the highest aspirations expressed as counterpoints to the straightjacket of a gloomy present.

Identifying Common Ground: We work toward a common future and try to keep the word consensus out of the discussion because it has too many other meanings. For ideals opposed by some but desired by others, we use the term "unresolved differences." We seek to separate the ideals ("what" people want) on a common futures list from *potential projects* ("how" to get there), and we have added a third list, *unresolved differences*, to acknowledge reality. (We don't homogenize or polarize the views expressed). We involve the whole group in making these lists rather than a task force or a few observers.

Action Planning: We like to do action planning in two phases, based on personal responsibility (not recommendations to others), typically in stakeholder groups first, then voluntary task forces.

Note: These are our preferences, not prescriptions. We may change our instructions or vocabulary for specific tasks, or where cultural and language differences require it. We pay attention to the context. We stay aware that words are tricky and may mean quite different things to different people in the room. That is why we are reluctant to supply categories to organize the content people produce, preferring to let a group struggle with confirming meanings with each other.

creative, fanciful, or serious, linear, and data-laden. At this point, people often rise to the heights of aspiration and idealism, the polar opposite of where they were a day earlier. After observing all the scenarios, the whole conference in mixed groups notes *common future* themes (what people want), *potential projects* (how to get there), and what they see as *unresolved differences* (key disagreements that may remain). The lists are made by each group, then merged with other groups' lists and posted on the wall. Usually there is 80% or more overlap. Groups have as much time as they wish, most taking up to an hour, after which they are done for the day.

Day 3 – Morning

First thing in the morning the whole group reviews the lists again. A discussion follows on what we really mean by this or that statement. If we cannot agree on a value or feature of our common future, the conflict is not "worked." We simply recognize who supports what and put the item on the appropriate list. Everybody knows where the others stand.

"Even though there were a lot of disagreements, we still ended up with a consensus that we need to work on that and find solutions."

The ground rule is that we report the lists as understood in light of everything that's been learned in the past two days. Anything that stirs up disagreement is reported as "unresolved difference" endorsed by some, not all. In this task we explore the tension between the ideal and the actual. People experience a choice between repeating old patterns and taking new paths. They must decide whether to replay the conflicts that persist at the cost of working the newly-discovered common ground, or to work *on* common ground without resolving every issue. They are learning that they can't do both now. There are only a few hours to decide on the next steps.

We now have from three to five hours for action planning. Stakeholder and/or self-selected groups make short- and long-range action plans for implementing their ideal future. People have a chance to "put a stake in the ground" and invite others who have energy for a particular project or theme to join them. They report to the conference before closing, and

make plans for disseminating the outcomes.

In this task we are creating opportunities for people to collaborate across boundaries. Once they decide on their goals and commit to next steps, they are likely to sustain the energy to involve others and stay connected.

The conference closes between noon and 3 pm on Day 3.

Making Choices

The future search conference puts people in a position of having to choose, as a temporary planning community, which way to go now. They have no authorities telling them what to think or do about their discoveries. They have little choice except to fight, abandon the task, or deal with each other in a new way. Our goal in running this meeting is to hold the task front and center in such a way that people must deal with each other in order to deal with it.

Cutting loose old ways of relating is no small feat. It opens doors to new experiences. When we suspend the sense of security engendered by reducing uncertainty to simple problems, we free ourselves to make more creative choices. We open up common ground none of us knew existed. This trip into unknown territory can be made because everyone works on tasks of mutual concern. When people accept the conference task, they are more likely to work together despite their skepticism, gloomy predictions, blind faith in leaders and experts, and other "shadows" that may hound any of us.

Riding the Roller Coaster

The task structure outlined here may produce information overload and heighten confusion. Facing such complexity alone, many people feel impotent; they would be overwhelmed if they weren't in company with a lot of other stakeholders. To understand a future search it's not enough to know there are five tasks. You need to appreciate that each task has a dynamic potential, analogous to particular moments on a roller-coaster. Taking the ride together leads to

widely-supported action on common ground. We like the metaphor because it captures the ups and downs of the event.

The dynamic process can be visualized this way:

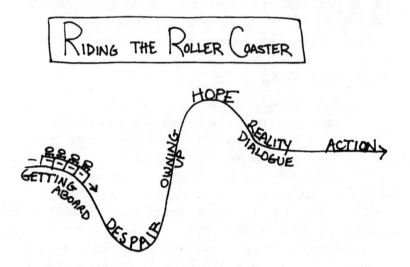

• **Getting Aboard.** People come aboard with their own experience – of themselves, their world, and the future search topic. Whether oriented toward "facts" or "feelings" or both, they soon find they can relate to strangers and even adversaries through their mutual experiences.

• **Plunging to the Depths.** After they establish their common world and connectedness, they face a complex mess that seems out of their control. They may plunge towards denial, fear, gloom, challenge, hopelessness, even impotence. The dominant mood becomes, "It's a mess!"

• **Owning Up.** As folks accept what they are doing, want to do, and how they feel about it, they discover that "*we* are all we've got." They encounter what's working and what isn't and begin a climb out of despair. Now, the mood changes and people may say, "It's our mess!"

• **Rising to the Heights.** People enact their ideals and discover attractive futures. They create portraits of the world they really want as if they already have it. They become energized and excited.

• **Dialoguing About Real Choices.** The group faces a choice. Will they act now on common ground or put their energy into the differences and problems that remain as a way out? People vacillate between talking and acting as they confront the reality that the world is neither all bad nor all good. It's as if the roller-coaster has a throttle and a brake, and the riders are using both at the same time. The choice is between going back towards familiar (and unsatisfying) patterns and inching towards an unknown (and attractive) future. Agreeing to work on common futures despite unresolved differences is a transforming step. Many groups conclude, *"This is the best we can do now!"* That's a priceless insight. It enables people to take back control of their world, feel more secure in their planning, and gain greater support for their visions.

• **Taking Responsibility.** Running a future search conference means accepting these critical dynamic ups and downs. For sponsors and steering committee members, the pre-conference dialogue often mirrors this dynamic. Once the decision is made to go forward, the other processes follow from our design. Consultants and facilitators need to learn how to manage the whole ride – in the meetings and in themselves. Conference sponsors will benefit from understanding that putting conflicts on hold does not exempt them from anxious moments. Indeed, without these moments, we would have no change worth having.

"It was an emotional roller-coaster in a sense. You come in expecting great things and you hear some things that are really discouraging.... Then you see people come together and start working on solutions to problems that are identified."

FACILITIATING THE ROLLER-COASTER RIDE

CONFERENCE DYNAMICS	WHAT WE DO
Getting Aboard **(Review of the Past)**	We set up norms of task, time, and the validity of all ideas.
Plunging to the Depths **(Mind-Map of Present)**	We stay with the dominant mood.
Owning Up **(Prouds & Sorries)**	We encourage people taking ownership.
View from the Heights **(Ideal Futures)**	We don't pat ourselves on the back for the good feelings. We're not finished yet.
Dialogue About **Real Choices** **(Common Future)**	We point out the choice between reworking old ground or moving toward new actIon plans.

CHAPTER 2

Future Search In Action

Learning from Experience

> "No one can force change on anyone else.
> It has to be experienced. Unless we invent
> ways where paradigm shifts can be
> experienced by large numbers of people,
> then change will remain a myth."
>
> – Eric Trist

MANY ORGANIZATIONS AND COMMUNITIES are learning how to engage large numbers of people in experiencing themselves as part of a larger whole. For people lucky enough to have this experience, "change" is no longer a myth or buzzword, but a shared reality. Future search, as a way of working in this context, seems both promising and challenging. As we catalogue the experiences of hundreds of participants and facilitators, we find that:

1. The future search method is learnable. A great many people have run these conferences with integrity. Self-confidence grows with each new experience.

2. The uses are limited only by our alertness to opportunities, imagination, and persistence. Folks have run conferences in a wide variety of organizations and communities, and in many cultures.

3. People who succeed with future search have in common a focus on the minimum conditions for success, the ability to pick promising situations, and the courage to act.

The examples below are typical of hundreds of future search conferences run across North America and abroad. All the folks named here are members of SearchNet, our community service network. Many of these examples are covered in detail in a case book published by SearchNet (Weisbord et al, 1994).

Implementing a City-Wide Consensus

"When I came in I was curious and anxious. What are we going through? How will we get any answers? We got more answers than I thought we were going to get."

The *Aligning for Action* Conference in Kansas City in November 1993 showed how future search could be used to implement a community consensus reached earlier. Citizens of the Greater Kansas City area agreed they wanted to become "The Child Opportunity Capital." Indeed, Kansas City Consensus and its executive director, Tammy Blossom, had sponsored a multi-year process to mobilize agreement around five goal areas relative to children – families, neighborhoods, jobs, education, and cooperation across all boundaries. While thousands of citizens were involved, they had no good way to link goals, neighborhoods, and local governments. "People will not sit still for another 'planning' meeting," said Blossom. "They want action – now."

Nancy Aronson and Beverly Arsht, consultants to Kansas City Consensus, teamed with Carole Cohn and John VanDeusen, of the Philadelphia SearchNet project. Two parallel *implementation* conferences were run, each with 65 folks from every sector, neighborhood, and goal area – a diverse cross section of Greater Kansas City. "It would be hard to overstate the complexity of the issues we dealt with in two and a half days," wrote Blossom and Marcus Jackson, President of Kansas City Consensus.

Ten action teams set time lines and goals for funding, youth empowerment, services integration, and regional col-

laboration, using technology, volunteer youth programs (linked to National Service). Within weeks a deputy juvenile officer was placed at a local high school which had tried for a year to get more student services through normal channels. Children's Mercy Hospital put young people on boards dealing with hospital oversight and procedures, a direct result of a conference consensus on including youth in substantive forums. In March 1994 a local Junior League chose the youth empowerment project as its next four year community commitment. The offer included 90 volunteers and a $200,000 activities grant including an annual future search involving young people.

Union/Management Joint Planning

"Plant Engineering 2004: Unity through Partnership" was the theme for a future search held by 3M Company's St. Paul Area Plant Engineering organization as part of an ongoing effort to improve work methods, morale, quality of work life, productivity, and management practice. Internal consultants Paul Pelkola and Bob Boyd organized and ran the conference with Sandra. "Getting the workers, managers, executives, union officials, and customers all in one room to shape our organization was like a pipe dream," said Pelkola, "but I became convinced there was no other way." Union/management tensions had always made joint improvement efforts difficult. Management worried that they would lose control if they got into an open discussion with union and other stakeholders. Union officials worried that their credibility

with the rank and file would be tainted if they appeared too collaborative.

At the same time, management wanted the union to understand the company's situation, and the union thought the conference might help in the negotiating process. It was a big step for both sides. To their mutual benefit, they produced a joint vision of a workplace redesigned around customer needs. They also devised processes for including people who did not attend to be implemented by conference participants. As a result, Plant Engineering moved into a large-scale redesign effort, union and management working together, that included hundreds of employees.

Organizing State-Wide Voluntary Action

A Pennsylvania affiliate of the national Children's Literacy Initiative had funding for a state chapter but lacked a way to involve the right parties. Bill Moon and Loretta Raider helped convene a future search for 60 state and local officials, librarians, day care workers, Head Start staff, foundation executives, school teachers, principals, and bookstore owners. They forged a Children's Literacy Council for Pennsylvania, linking public schools, Head Start programs and other stakeholders separated for decades despite common concerns. Their goal is to have all preschool children statewide ready to read by the time they start school. They began meeting quarterly, working on such issues as funding, providing books, and training librarians to help care-givers learn to read aloud with children.

Regional Economic Development

In 1992, the Inuit people of the Arctic region negotiated a new homeland, Nunavut, with the Canadian government. It is an area seven times the size of Texas with 22,000 residents. To establish a strategic development framework, a leading Inuit economic development organization sponsored a future search for participants from 25 widely-scattered settle-

ments, Inuit land claims organizations, territorial and federal governments, banks, business firms and organizations, a mining company, aboriginal funding organizations, and members of other aboriginal organizations.

Inuit Invitation

Mike Bell, a consultant from Yellowknife, facilitated the conference. Groups worked and presented material in either Inuktitut, the aboriginal language, or English, with instant translation. Key flip charts were written in both languages. The conference had unique cultural features such as Inuit drum dancing and traditional hand games and sports during

coffee breaks. Local school children from Rankin Inlet, the meeting site, sat in and several participated in skits describing Nunavut in 2010. "We can adapt this model," said Bell, who has worked all over he world, "for many different cultures."

The conference produced an economic development framework and action plan for education and training, social development, preservation of culture and language, development of small business and industry, investments, organizational development, transportation and infrastructure, renewable resource development, and protection of the environment.

Rethinking Work Systems

Using future search principles, many organizations have gone from scratch to the implementation of new work systems in about a third as much time as it took in the 1980's. One notable example is the work of Dick and Emily Axelrod with the Hudson Division of R.R. Donnelley and Sons Company, where a traditional factory transformed into a team-based organization with the help of employees from all levels, customers, and company staff. A series of conferences based on future search made possible a common understanding of how the whole system works, and gave separate departments insight into how they affected each others' work. The new design led to increased teamwork, better customer service and quality, and lower costs.

Community Development

Hopkinton, MA, a town of 9000, more than doubled in size between 1977 and 1992. A tax-limiting referendum left education and other budgets level-funded for three years, despite 6 percent a year inflation that wiped out contractual raises for school employees. Janice Williams, a resident, ran a future search conference, "Hopkinton 2002 AD," that included citizens, commissioners, police, fire, highway, water and other department heads, business leaders, teachers, stu-

dents, school administrators – all the folks with a stake in the community.

They made two major commitments. One, they would preserve the rural character of the town (25 miles west of Boston), keeping it attractive to newcomers while managing its rapid growth. To do this, the town funded a government committee to create a town-wide strategic plan. Two, they would preserve and improve the quality of the local school system.

At a subsequent town meeting residents raised their school budget 12 percent, a trend that continued for three years, restoring cuts in staff and programs. Within a year of the conference, a local business firm formed a partnership with the high school, donated $350,000 worth of computers, technology, and teacher training, and $300,000 more was pledged for the next two years.

Rethinking Business Strategy

Gil Steil managed his first future search at Digital Equipment Corporation when he was an internal consultant. "The Future of Imaging at Digital" led to the development of a single strategic plan for a new technology where only days earlier there had been five competing plans." When the strategy task force spawned by the conference completed their work two weeks later," reported Steil, "we re-convened the whole community to refine the task force work and get larger buy-in and commitment." They had learned that "the implementation of common ground was a whole lot easier than the resolution of conflict."

Building Relationships Across Urban Cultures

In Philadelphia, Museums in the Life of a City – the Initiative for Cultural Pluralism – wanted a shared vision and action plan to link inner city communities and museums. To this end, Marilyn Sifford and Carole Cohn ran a future search in 1992. Stakeholders included community members, leaders

of business, government, the arts, museums, and diverse funding agencies.

Participants saw culture and the arts as central to lifelong learning and envisioned ongoing partnerships between museums and neighborhoods to promote cultural inclusion. "The challenge," wrote Cynthia Primas and Portia Hamilton-Sperr, executives of Museums in the Life of a City, "is whether together we can build a vision of the city in more detail; a place that will be attractive to experience, where art and culture will be widely distributed..." The conference organized five task forces – on regionalism in greater Philadelphia, partnerships between organizations, cultural institutions as neighborhood centers, strategic planning for cultural organizations, and arts and culture as both community and economic development.

"So, for me, did the future search work? No question about it. It provided, I think, a very living model of democracy that doesn't currently exist in this country."

State-Wide Political Action

For three years the Massachusetts legislature debated measures to create an extension service that would help manufacturers become more competitive. Then in December 1992 a statewide future search conference run by Sandra made service a centerpiece of a common future scenario. It won support from business owners, public and private service providers, legislators, and US Senator John Kerry.

Eight weeks after the future search, following intensive lobbying by participants, the bill passed with a $1 million budget. The extension service would do for manufacturers what agricultural extension has done for farmers. "A lot of peoples' thinking and interest were galvanized in the conference," said John Hoops, head of Bay State Skills Corporation's Industrial Modernization Program, a key conference sponsor. The plan became one of 12 key action items on the governor's agenda.

"It was really incredible," recalled Leslie Schneider, a co-sponsor from Tufts University's Center for Technology, "to see everyone show up, be in a room for three days, and listen to each other in a way they never had before. The public

forum was important. We all got the same story from the same people at the same time." Four months later participants held a "reunion" to present their report to Senator Kerry and Governor Weld, who announced the new integrated state service. Said one manufacturer, "What it took us seven years to do in the Berkshire Plastics Network, we did here in 16 hours!" In 1994 an additional $10 million was earmarked to support the program.

S'organiser Pour Le Futur (Organizing for the Future)

Alcan Smelters & Chemicals Ltd. (SECAL), a division of Alcan Aluminum Company, wanted to identify how the smelting facilities should be organized in the next century. Jean Pierre Beaulieu and Emile Carriere, their consultants,

ran a future search to envision a new production organization in the year 2005. SECAL invited people from corporate, all plants, community, suppliers and customers to participate, on the assumption that a common vision of a future production facility could start existing plants moving in that direction. Participants used a special French version of the future search design and vocabulary adapted by the consultants.

Two broad themes evolved: a greater focus on the individual as a major contributor and a commitment to build partnerships with stakeholders, particularly unions, customers, suppliers, and the community. Action ideas included concrete steps for realigning corporate headquarters and specialized staff roles, continuous training, and a zero accident work environment. A major outcome was a shared vision of what a new plant should be and what types of skills should be developed for the next century.

Board/Staff Relations

Board members and staff have made major shifts in their relationships in future searches. One notable example was a conference we helped organize for The Alliance for Employee Growth and Development, a non-profit joint venture of the Communications Workers of America, the International Brotherhood of Electrical Workers, and AT&T. Their mission is empowering AT&T employees displaced by technology to develop new careers. The Board – senior executives from the three partners – found, to their surprise, that local committees around the United States resented having little board contact. They decided to combine board meetings with site visits around the country, giving all parties first-hand, ongoing information on the state of The Alliance. These visits are run on future search principles. In addition, when The Alliance goes into a community, they convene local employers, government, education, and social services to help them make action plans.

Bangladesh, a largely Moslem nation of 110 million, will double its population in 25 years in an area the size of Wisconsin. Population problems, malnutrition, illiteracy, and poverty are endemic. Kathryn Esty, a Massachusetts-based consultant working with UNICEF, discovered there "a real hunger for new ways to help people talk to each other across groups, sectors, and ideologies." When she proposed training Bangladeshis to organize their own future searches, the idea quickly caught on. Rolf Carriere, local head of UNICEF, agreed to sponsor an experimental workshop. "We were not sure," reported Esty, "how transferable the future search conference methodology would be to a country with such a minimal tradition of participation. We wondered too if the enormity of problems in Bangladesh would impact the appropriateness of the methodology."

In the fall of 1994, Esty and Gil Steil ran a simulation for 50 Bangladeshi consultants, trainers, and managers, using as their topic "The Future of the Children of Dhaka." They learned several important lessons. The method was readily accepted by Bangladeshis, who joined in with enthusiasm. At the same time, so great are the nation's problems that people had trouble dreaming large future dreams. "For example," wrote Esty, "many participants could not envision their city without child labor, even by the year 2014. The most they could hope for was 'less child labor.' Reflecting on this, most participants agreed with the man who said, 'We need to learn how to dream.'" Several potential follow-up conferences were discussed. The most immediate application was aimed at rethinking a way to combat diarrhea, which kills 250,000 children in Bangladesh each year.

WHAT WE CAN'T DO WITH FUTURE SEARCH

While the above are fine success stories, we have learned some hard lessons attempting future search conferences under negative conditions. There are several things we don't know how to do.

Shore Up Ineffective Leaders

We cannot, for example, make up for weak leadership with a future search conference. Ten years ago a world-wide religious service organization's lawyer recruited Marvin to help them confront a drive by disgruntled central staff to unionize. A reluctant director went along with the "legal" advice to sponsor a future search that would enable people to devise the workplace they wanted. It was a big success in the sense that folks welcomed a chance to interact and make new plans. They were not surprised when the boss acted on none of them. Nor was their attorney surprised when the staff voted in a union to fill the leadership vacuum.

Convince Skeptics to Go Forward

We have had no success "selling" future search conferences to skeptics or folks paralyzed by worry about losing control. One troubled corporate giant planned to put thousands of people through a training event staged by a prestigious business institute, incorporating every new idea on customers, markets, service, and empowerment. To the proposal of several staff that the company substitute future searches – on the theory that people could get the company out of the box if given a chance – top management turned a deaf ear. Nobody could imagine anything useful happening that wasn't prescribed by experts. The chance that people might *do* exactly what was needed, or that collectively they had enough skills and knowledge, was far outside the frame of reference in the executive suite.

They opted for expert training. But nobody got empowered. No new markets opened up, no customers came flock-

ing to the gates, and service did not get better. Having only two years to "transform the culture or die," they gave up on training their way out of trouble after a year. Several separate departments ran successful future searches, but the company as a whole continued its downward slide.

Reconcile Values Differences

We don't know how to reconcile intractable values differences through future search. When people disagree about deep-seated religious, ethical, or political beliefs which they hold sacred, a future search is unlikely to help them reconcile their beliefs. The choice they face is whether to accept their differences and work together on common ground despite them, or to work in opposition. Indeed, in a future search, we are helping people do what they already agree on and have never been able to do because they spend so much time fighting about matters they cannot resolve.

In a school conference people brought up some highly-charged feelings about sex education. The differences between those who did and did not want a particular curriculum were fierce, deeply felt, and long standing. The parties simply believed each other to be wrong. At the same time, they agreed on a host of other goals, like better use of school facilities and more involvement of parents and the business community in learning and teaching. They discovered they were not going to work out their moral values in this forum. They also saw a priceless chance to make real progress on matters of benefit to all if they agreed to cooperate.

Change Team Dynamics with Future Search Technology

We can create new dynamics quickly only if we bring together a new group and give it a new task. Systems expert Russell Ackoff (1974) pointed out long ago that systems change only in relation to the larger systems of which they are a part. That explains why peer-only events – training, T-groups, team meetings – have little effect on the larger

system. So our guiding principle, when we make out a future search invitation list, is: We want the "whole system" in the room, meaning a larger system than usual.

Using future search work sheets, for example, a consultant ran a single department through the event – past, present, and future, the works. However, uneasy that the boss was reluctant to invite outside stakeholders, and to make sure everybody "got it," she included a trust questionnaire and data feedback, and made building trust an explicit goal. "Same old stuff," was the word after the conference, from the same people who neither trusted nor distrusted each other any more after the conference than before, although they had learned to trust consultants less. Same people = same interactions.

LEARNING FROM EXPERIENCE

We end this chapter with a summary of what we've learned about increasing the chances for a successful future search. This is not to say you can't do anything if you miss one or more of these points. None are all-or-nothing propositions, just tips and traps to keep you thinking about what it takes to deliver on what you promise.

Tips

A future search will be more effective when:

1. We present it as a milestone at a choice point in a community's or organization's life;
2. We seek to involve large numbers of diverse people;
3. Top managers and/or community leaders are involved and have a deep wish to succeed with this event;
4. Participants include a cross-section of groups with a stake in the focal issue or community, or of functions, levels, and "outside" stakeholders like customers, suppliers, government officials, and community members;

5. Participants manage information, analysis and action planning themselves;
6. We focus broadly on opportunities, not narrowly on specific problems;
7. Facilitators stay out of the way when people are working productively, and become active when there is conflict or avoidance of tasks;
8. We validate everybody's reality as legitimate and deserving to be heard. We do not seek to edit, rewrite, or bury any statement.

Traps

A future search may fall flat if:

1. Too few people – diverse groups make for more opportunities;
2. Too little stakeholder variety – we need many viewpoints/actors;
3. Featured keynote speakers or presenters. That changes the tone and dynamics of the meeting away from shared views of participants. We want people to accept responsibility for their own plans;
4. The emphasis shifts from appreciating what is and what could be to bemoaning past and present problems;
5. The group recreates unresolved conflicts or shirks the assigned tasks;
6. Leaders don't support initiatives that come out of the conference or use the opportunity to speak for their own vision;
7. Consultants seek to diagnose and fill a group's needs, or preempt time for training (e.g. style instruments, surveys, skill exercises, group games). This shifts control from participants to an external source, depriving the group of responsibility.

CHAPTER 3

Conditions for Success

> "The unconscious is continually active, combining its material in ways which serve the future. It produces, no less than the conscious mind, subliminal combinations that are prospective; only they are markedly superior to the conscious combinations both in refinement and in scope. For these reasons the unconscious could serve man as a unique guide, provided that he can resist the lure of being misguided."
>
> – C.G. Jung

IN THIS CHAPTER WE DISCUSS eight "conditions for success" that we encourage conference planners to apply. They embody what we have learned about the art of finding common ground in diverse groups. We seek these conditions for conferences we manage because they make sense to us and are confirmed by many colleagues around the world.

The cynicism folks express about meetings is reinforced when we use shortcuts that are *not* equal to the outcomes sought. We still get a lot of pressure to do that. We are often asked to run shorter events with less diversity in basement dungeon rooms, attendance optional, featuring a preconceived agenda. These conditions fall far short of what we want to do within a future search. It is no service to a conference sponsor to pretend that using some of our tasks and techniques will meet aspirations for breakthroughs if we

compromise key conditions that are much more important than our procedures.

Simple, not easy

We do not mean to imply that if we stick to our guns this becomes easy work or that 16+ hours makes up for years of inertia or conflict. Planning how to get the right people in the room is hard work. And future search methods are so straight-forward as to be easily dismissed. Yet they are profound enough to create great anxiety in us about control, conflict, and failure. It is reassuring to know that the basics for success come from decades of experience in many cultures, documented in *Discovering Common Ground* (Weisbord et al, 1992).

People skilled in group dynamics can succeed by adhering to the conditions outlined below. Those who can do this while containing their own anxiety about success and failure, may surprise themselves with the productivity of the community they have helped bring to life.

CONDITIONS FOR SUCCESS

- "Whole system" in the room
- Global context, local action
- Common ground and future focus,
 not problems and conflicts
- Self-managed small groups
- Full attendance
- Healthy meeting conditions
- 3 day event (i.e. "sleep twice")
- Public responsibility for follow-up

Let's take up each condition in turn.

Getting the "whole system" in the room

We need a broad cross-section of stakeholders for several reasons. First, we want diverse perceptions so that everyone can get a new picture of the whole. One function or level of an

organization can't learn enough about the world *or* itself in a closed meeting. Second, we want to encourage the forming of as many new relationships as possible. Each participant opens up many different kinds of action possibilities. So the more diverse the attendees, the greater will be the innovation and the potential for shared implementation. We need people with ideas, people with authority to act, people we want to influence, people with special skills and creativity, all with a stake in the future search task.

In community conferences, we have to consider a cross section of all sectors the sponsors consider relevant. No two lists are alike. For example, here is the invitation list for "Bringing Manufacturing Back to America" held in Santa Clara, California in January 1994:

- Education (8 people)
- Government (17)
- Small and Large Manufacturers (24)
- Labor (8)
- Community Organizations (8)
- Economic Development (8)
- Business Associations (8)

In future searches sponsored by a single organization, we seek 25 percent to 40 percent of the group from "outside" stakeholders – e.g. customers, suppliers, government officials, headquarters staff, community – key people who don't normally work together. This translates into two or three "outside" stakeholders at each mixed table. Here's a computer network service company's stakeholder list:

- Advisers (8 people)
- Customers (8)
- Market Technologists (8)
- Management (8)
- Contract Employees (8)
- Company Staff (8)
- Customer Service (8)
- Family Members (8)

Of course we never do get the *whole* system in the room. Taken literally, that would mean every organism in the cosmos. However, we can *always* get a diagonal slice. We find 60 – 70 stakeholders is optimum, providing ample diversity. We base this limit in part on how large a group dialogue we can manage. We've found that when the group numbers in the high 70's and beyond, face-to-face dialogue, a central tenet of our work, becomes harder – you can't see the faces of people at the other end of the room; you can't hear without an audio system. Also small group reports must be shorter because there are so many of them; the shorter the report, the more discussion time people require to formulate it. The more discussion time spent in small groups, the less is available for the whole community. And so on.

Our limit may seem arbitrary and certainly can be tested. We have used our model in groups numbering from 30 to 100, and 64 or fewer is what we like best. When more folks must be involved, we recommend sequential conferences. It would be wise to run several single conferences before taking on a large systems change strategy utilizing future search. We avoid parallel conferences, though many folks are experimenting with them, because of the logistical complexity. Few sponsors can invest the extra time and resources needed to insure the success of such events.

"I'm pretty active in the community. So to come to this event and find two-thirds of the participants doing a future search and me not know them was very provocative, very exciting."

Thinking globally, acting locally

Rather than study only our conference entity, we look at our task in reference to society as a whole. We explore trends *within and between* the search entity *and* the world outside – the entire "open system." Thus, we explore our participants' views of *global* trends as a backdrop to the community, institution, sector, or company under study. All the trends affecting stakeholders in the room right now are mapped as *they* see them. This procedure goes hand-in-hand with diversity – the more stakeholders, the broader their shared world view. Putting local issues in global perspective, they are less likely to fight over or avoid the issues.

There is no mystery about why and how we discuss some themes and not others – somebody in the room saw fit to include them. Individually, we remember bits and pieces of our past. Together, we remember a whole lot more.

Exploring current reality and common futures, not problems and conflicts

We invest in ideal future scenarios (5-20 years out) rather than problem-solving or conflict-management. We acknowledge but do not "work" differences. This is *not* a team-building meeting, in which people negotiate new relationships, sharpen interpersonal skills, and solve past problems. Instead, we reserve a big block of time for imaginatively inventing new futures and dramatizing them. Common ground on the future forms the backdrop for action planning. The transformative experience includes discovering what's possible at the very moment we can act.

Self-managed explorations and action plans

We use self-managing small groups, where *everybody* shares information, interprets it, decides action steps. These groups reduce hierarchy, passivity, conflict, and dependency on experts *or* facilitators. When they succeed, people experience discovery, learning, and cooperation. We avoid long speeches, expert presentations, and exercises, instruments, or games based on external diagnoses of what this group needs. Nor do we organize data or coordinate follow-up plans. We recommend that small groups divide up the work among a discussion leader, recorder, reporter, time keeper and data manager, and that people rotate roles. This greatly increases the chance for every person to have a leadership role. This is not obvious to participants, although it makes a major shift in a group's relationship to authority. Our aim is to shift the locus of control from external sources to the group itself.

"It was a more open, intellectu-ally-challenging environment than I had been in, some of these planning exercises I'd been through before."

Attending the whole meeting

People need to stay engaged to achieve the perceptual shift that changes their capacity for action. Moreover, they can't act if they aren't there and others can't influence them, making it certain people will hold on to their stereotypes and fantasies of the absent parties. Innovative planning on common ground requires a fully shared experience. It's harder for folks to join in a common future if they missed important steps taken in arriving at it. We discourage non-stakeholder observers. If there are strong reasons for having non-participants present, find something useful for them to do, like documenting the conference.

Meeting under healthy conditions

Daylight (windows) and good food are important for optimum work. Choosing to spend three days in poorly-lit, interior spaces with the wrong diet/snacks is a bad economic *and* social decision, no matter how worthy the agenda. We choose airy rooms with windows, plan lighter lunches, and have nutritious snacks available to keep up peoples' energy.

Working across 3 days (i.e. "sleep twice")

Two days, even long ones, won't do as well as 2 1/2 days for a future search. It's not the total hours worked, but the spacing of learning – the "soak time" – that leads us to understand each other's views, fully accept the high and low points, and do new things together. For example, we schedule from lunch on Day 1 to early afternoon on Day 3. Other formats are possible – a late afternoon session on Day 1, or a long evening session. However, our evening break points are not arbitrary. We want to break in the middle of important tasks so that people stay engaged over night. The unconscious works in mysterious ways on unfinished business. We want to give this process a chance to work out. In conferences run for two full days, action planning comes at exactly the

wrong time – when people are overloaded and tired.

We are convinced the shift in group capability for future action and implementation is *much* greater in "two sleep" than in shorter conferences. (If you want a research project, here's a hypothesis crying to be tested.) Also the burden on leaders and consultants is less. There will be fewer loose ends hanging out, many more initiatives taken, less dependency and waiting for somebody else to act, and much faster implementation.

Taking responsibility publicly for follow-up

When we publicly declare our intentions to take next steps we are more likely to follow through. Kurt Lewin, the "practical theorist," discovered this principle in the famous food habit studies during World War II that led to the emergence of "participative management" (Weisbord, 1987, Chapter 3). So we ask people to say publicly what they, themselves, will do next. We ask them to sign up for action groups rather than put the ball back in the sponsor's court.

THE PRESSURE TO COMPROMISE IN THE PLANNING

We cannot have change without tackling something new. At the same time, we resist the unfamiliar. People sometimes argue they want a future search but "don't have time" for the whole agenda. Actually, we think our complete meeting runs on a pretty fast track, and anybody who tries to speed it up still more probably has a different agenda than planning breakthroughs. If a conference falls short of the mark, and you have been the spark plug, people will end up blaming :

(a) fate,
(b) each other,
(c) you.

"What I heard most from people, who are typically disenfranchised in our community, was their surprise at hearing that other people actually care about the same issues...and were willing to take action."

The right answer is (c) you. You promised a moon walk, then agreed to a scheme that gets folks only as far as the launch pad.

For most future search sponsors, the breakthroughs are made before the conference – in the commitment of setting aside enough time, inviting a cross-section of people who never meet, and getting everybody to stay for the whole meeting. In short, the big change happens in the planning session. It can only happen if the steering group (see Chapter 6) agrees to a set of conditions different from the norm. The closer a conference matches all eight conditions for success, the more likely we are to put aside stereotypes and prejudices and act together. Too many compromises and we get back to business-as-usual. A good test of any system's ability to change is how it schedules its time. If people can't spare the hours, or insist on part-time attendance, you had best take Nancy Reagan's advice. Just say no.

Good Reasons for Skepticism

And you *will* be pressured to compromise. There are lots of reasons for pre-conference jitters. Most people have yet to work this way. Outcomes cannot be predicted, and there are no guarantees. Still, we know from abundant reports that a future search experience is likely to be renewing, productive, idealistic, practical, and surprisingly long-lasting. Nobody believes this when they plan a conference. Along the way we face lots of ambiguity. No wonder, then, that potential sponsors sometimes get cold feet contemplating the very components essential for success: broad base of stakeholders, for example, which means inviting people who don't usually meet; or visiting the *global* context before confronting our local planning issue; or working in self-managing peer groups, including strangers and people who have a history of conflict or failure; or meeting for 16 hours (excluding breaks and meals) over three days instead of trying to squeeze everything into one day; or delaying action planning until we have agreed on the nature of the future we all want. All these steps contribute to success.

G̲ROUND RULES

- ALL IDEAS ARE VALID
- EVERYTHING ON FLIP CHARTS
- LISTEN TO EACH OTHER
- OBSERVE TIME FRAMES
- SEEK COMMON GROUND & ACTION
 - NOT PROBLEMS & CONFLICTS

Some sponsors and planners assume *their* stakeholders are different. They won't show up, stay, or spend time talking about the past. They are too busy, too important, too knowledgeable to need a meeting like this, and even if they came, they would never agree on the future. These assumptions should be tested. Folks new to future search may compromise key components before they have any experience, reducing both their anxiety and a chance for anything new to happen.

Keep in mind that when we hold to the basics we can make key breakthroughs. Be aware that much larger or much smaller groups, with little diversity of backgrounds and no interdependence, meeting in much shorter time frames constitute a different conference model, even if you use our worksheets. While there are many useful tasks that can be performed in other modes, we can't imagine replicating a future search without attending to the basics.

Finally, we repeat that our preferences – for time frames,

tasks, break points, and so on – are *one way* of embodying the success conditions. We believe our practices are internally-consistent. Above all, they work for us.

A Radical Stand Toward Conflict

A radical aspect of the future search conference is its stance toward conflict. If the right people show up, unresolved disagreements can almost always be found. Oftimes these are a natural outgrowth of the information generated. We encourage all viewpoints, yet discourage conferees from "working through" (trying to resolve) their differences. Instead, we try to create a figure/ground reversal, putting conflict on hold, and common stakes up front. In this way, people own up to and accept whatever issues emerge as real and relevant for determining common ground. We suggest people not try to change each others' minds and not work to reconcile opposites, only to admit their existence. We encourage people to express their differences so that everybody knows where they stand.

"You hear a lot of differences. I hear a lot of similarities."

We neither avoid nor confront the extremes. Rather, we put our energy into staking out the widest common ground that all can stand on. We urge people to resist compromise so that a shared perception of genuine common ground can emerge. It may grow wider or narrower as the discussion progresses. Then, from that realistic base, however broad or narrow, new forms of action become possible. People don't magically get better than they were. Rather, they tune in on different aspects of themselves – their more constructive and cooperative impulses.

At its best, future search can take the focus off personality and political differences, problems and symptoms and instead focus energy toward building a sustainable community.

Other Purposes, Other Structures

There are many activities that *could* utilize future search tasks, without embracing our purposes. The techniques don't care how they are used. Below we discuss meeting structures in which finding and acting on common ground are less likely than in a future search mode. All serve useful functions. However, we urge you not to confuse such meetings with a future search even though they might employ similar techniques.

- EMPLOYEE OR CITIZEN INVOLVEMENT
 TOWARD A PRECONCEIVED RESULT

Conferences called to ratify pre-existing decisions or solve problems by implementing a pre-defined plan may be necessary and important, but they have a different philosophic base from getting everybody to take responsibility for the whole. In complementary fashion, a future search may be a good vehicle for creating implementation plans for a vision already widely-shared – so long as conferees have a hand in deciding what to do and how.

- SINGLE UNIT OR ONE TEAM CONFERENCES

Rather than holding meetings for one function only (e.g. human resource staff, manufacturing, sales), we include a mix of customers, clients, community, and government to provide broader perspectives on the issues. We want them there to influence and to be influenced toward appropriate action. An established work group, whether based in a factory or a board room, will usually act out the same old on-site dynamics when meeting at the Holiday Inn.

- EXPERT OR TOP DOWN SPEECHES
 OR TV TOWN MEETINGS

Expert talks followed by group discussion or question-and-answer is a worthwhile activity, widely-used, and well understood. However, this kind of meeting does not fulfill the basic conditions for a dialogue of discovery and voluntary action planning. Its purpose is only to influence by

providing information, a relatively weak strategy for building collaborative action.

• GETTING INPUT WITHOUT ACTING IN "REAL TIME"

The culture of business tends to overvalue "collecting data" or "getting input" in advance while excluding from the meeting those who supplied it. A future search is not a meeting to "get input" so that a hierarchy or central staff can create a future vision. What makes future search unique is that the output is seen to belong to everyone from the start.

• TASK FORCE PROBLEM-SOLVING

A future search is not a problem-solving meeting, even if managed participatively. For example, if the conference task is to plan how to carry out a recycling program which nobody has bought into, it's probably not a search topic. What *might* fit is the future of environmental initiatives in the community, that could be used to influence recycling and also many other decisions.

• TEAM BUILDING, CONFLICT MANAGEMENT

While its methods can be used for this purpose, we don't think of a future search as a meeting where team-building is based on feedback about one another's behavior. Meetings to trade perceptions (e.g. projections, stereotypes) of various groups are excluded. The core of future search is establishing common ground – perceptions of shared dilemmas, experiences, world views, trends, etc. We want to elicit common hopes, fears, aspirations, and needs. Feelings *about* individuals or groups are not solicited though they may indeed be volunteered. If such comments raise tensions, we will hear peoples' reactions without seeking resolution. Sometimes conflicts dissolve and teams come together in these conferences – but people are not told that is what they must do.

• TRAINING EXERCISES, STRUCTURED ICE-BREAKERS, DIAGNOSTIC INSTRUMENTS, ETC.

While all of these reduce anxiety – the facilitators' and the participants' – none are necessary. They are based on different assumptions about what people need to act together.

Indeed, they may slow down the process of discovering common action possibilities, prolong group dependency, and distract people from the central task. It is important that facilitators learn that the anxiety people feel about the task is *functional* and *necessary* if we wish to encourage responsible, self-generated action.

Chapter 3

CONDITIONS
FOR SUCCESS

CHAPTER 4

Road Maps

Theory into Practice

> "There are many ways to understand life
> and the universe – through superstition,
> religion, philosophy, science, and so forth.
> While each approach has its own experts –
> scientists, priests, philosophers, doctors,
> poets – all are merely blind men receiving
> different impressions from touching the
> same elephant....From his own perspective,
> each expert's conclusion is knowledgeable
> and makes sense. Their theories, however,
> are merely parts of the whole picture. I, too,
> am one of the blind. And because I touch a
> different part of the elephant, I have devel-
> oped my own theory about the relationship
> of the universe to human life."
>
> – Lin Yun

IN THIS CHAPTER WE SURVEY some views of the elephant
called "whole systems" that make sense to us in designing
meetings. These are far from all the possible theories we
could bring to bear. In effect, we are blind too. We use ideas
that resonate in us. We want to highlight the "road maps"
that have contributed to our understanding of how to orga-
nize a future search.

The future search design evolved not from any wish to use
particular techniques. Rather, it came from our desire to find
ways to involve large numbers of people in improving whole
systems. We wanted methods equal to our aspirations; more,
we wanted methods that affirm the dignity of each person,

faithful to the spirit of democracy. Since the coining of the phrase "group dynamics" more than 50 years ago, people have experimented with how to involve large groups in productive tasks. Until recently, though, this learning – captured in the phrase "participative management" – was applied largely through problem-solving task forces or natural work teams. This mode sought to honor democracy by including people in solving their own problems. It did not assure that the problems solved would benefit a whole system. Quite the opposite. When each of us works on our preferred problem, we tend to ignore, deny, or downplay everybody else's.

To counteract this trend, many people have in the last 30 years brought "systems thinking" into planning meetings. Most often it's in the form of systems models and maps used by small groups of expert thinkers. While they produce sophisticated analyses of how problems are interconnected, systems experts often have a hard time getting ordinary people to grasp, let alone act on, their insights.

Our challenges in creating a future search design are two: to make the benefits of systems thinking available to everyone without having to teach systems analysis; to create settings in which people can work on their preferred problems under an umbrella of shared values and goals rather than at cross purposes. The building blocks we have used, part science, part art, part philosophy, part trial and error, can be traced back many dedades. We have integrated them into a meeting agenda based on research, theory, and intuition validated by experience. Increasingly, we believe that far from inventing something new we are rediscovering wisdom known for thousands of years in other cultures.

Two Key Perspectives

Still, we are children of our own culture. And our two main sources of inspiration come from parallel innovations in different parts of the English-speaking world. One was Eva Schindler-Rainman's and Ronald Lippitt's large-scale

FUTURE SEARCH BASICS

- "WHOLE SYSTEM" IN THE ROOM
- GLOBAL EXPLORATION BEFORE LOCAL ACTION
- FUTURE FOCUS AND COMMON GROUND
- SELF MANAGEMENT AND RESPONSIBILITY

community futures conferences in North America during the 1970's. Another was the pioneering work of Eric Trist, an Englishman, and Fred Emery, an Australian, in developing the Search Conference. (Hence the name *future search*.) From Schindler-Rainman and Lippitt we learned to get the whole system in the room and to focus on the future. From Trist and Emery we learned the importance of thinking globally before acting locally, and of having people manage their own planning. (See Weisbord et al, 1992.)

Each of these innovative practitioners designed a whole experience for a particular purpose, and we have done likewise. They have a shared value base in democratic ideals that underlie our work as well. Both sets have a common ancestor that is also ours – Kurt Lewin's field theory and action research – studying a situation in which we participate and assume responsibility. (G.W. Lewin, ed. 1948).

In addition, Sandra brings a systems perspective from her experiences in reorganizing experimental schools and in clinical groups. Marv brings decades of working through high-anxiety reorganizations in factories, offices, and research laboratories, in medical schools and in corporations.

Getting the Whole System in the Room and Focusing on the Future

The principles of getting the whole system in the room and focusing on the future derive from cases reported in *Productive Workplaces* (Weisbord, 1987). A key antecedent for this approach was the research by Schindler-Rainman and Lippitt (1980) on their community conferences in 88 cities, towns, and states. They found that bringing a cross-section of residents together in one room – sometimes as many as 250 people – led to breakthrough problem-solving, even in a day. Before the meeting, participants, like the blind men, imagined that the part of the elephant they touched defined the beast. When they pooled what they knew, each got a view of the whole more complete than any one had to begin with. This gave *everybody* an entirely new basis for planning.

Building on their work, we began involving as many stakeholder groups as we could – up to a dozen or more perspectives on the future search topic. The exact number was not important. What mattered was getting people from many parts of the "whole system" who did not normally interact. We discovered along the way that each different kind of person brings a new set of action possibilities. The mayor opens one door, the grass-roots activist another, the ordinary citizen still a third. Together, they make possible a range of commitments none could make alone. Leave any one out, and there is much less potential.

Lippitt and Schindler-Rainman *also* had concluded years before that problem-solving depresses people, whereas imagining ideal futures creates energy and optimism. A key feature of their conferences was inviting people to create "images of potential" (ideal futures) rather than go head-on at the problems. More, they evolved a method for bringing futures to life, asking people to visualize them as if they had already happened. These practices too we sought to build into our future search model.

A second key road map grew out of a historic strategic planning meeting for Bristol-Siddeley Aircraft Engine Co. in 1960 facilitated by Eric Trist and Fred Emery (Weisbord, et al, 1992, Chapter 2). Two cultures, jet engines and piston engines, had been forced into a merger by the British government. Now, they had to create one company and rethink their future. Emery proposed an agenda he thought would create "conditions for effective dialogue" based on the consensus research of social psychologist Solomon Asch (1952).

When people listen to each other and use concrete examples to back up their views, they get a much clearer picture of each others' reality and are more likely to have a dialogue leading to shared understandings. This discovery cannot be made in meetings where energy is focused on the leader's agenda, expert input, problem-solving differences, overcoming resistance, sweating over lack of data, or leaving responsibility with staff and hierarchy. From Asch, Emery extrapolated a set of "conditions for effective dialogue."

CONDITIONS FOR EFFECTIVE DIALOGUE
(EMERY, BASED ON ASCH)

(a) all parties are "talking about the same world," meaning that people back up their generalizations with concrete examples;

b) all human beings have basic psychological similarities, e.g. "laughing, loving, working, desiring, thinking, perceiving, etc." and if (a) and (b) happen, then –

(c) "the facts of one person's world become part of the other's" and they develop "a shared psychological field." At that point, people become capable of a genuine dialogue on what to do. A successful dialogue depended on how much the parties perceived increased freedom of choice along with greater understanding. If they did, reasoned Emery, then we could assume that –

(d) they will experience their common dilemmas and/ or shared fate and plan accordingly.

Emery embraced Asch's insight that, "Consensus is valid only to the extent to which each individual asserts his own relation to facts and retains his individuality; there can be no genuine agreement...unless each adheres to the testimony of his experience and steadfastly maintains a hold on reality" (Weisbord et al, 1992, pp 21-23). Trist and Emery designed the Bristol-Siddeley merger meeting in part on Asch's research. They theorized that the two conflicting cultures would come together if they could experience their common context, psychological needs, and interdependent realities. Their innovation was to have the managers produce three kinds of data in sequence, in order to create the Asch conditions:

- Global Conditions
- Aircraft Industry
- Bristol and Siddeley Corporations

They asked the executives to put strategic planning in a global and industry-wide context. Next, they had them pool all they knew about both piston and jet engine markets, and explore the implications for a merged company. As students of group dynamics pioneeer Wilfred Bion, Trist and Emery expected people to fight, run away from the task, or look to the leaders for solutions. These were predictable dynamics in most task-focused meetings. Much to their surprise, they saw very little fight, flight, or dependency in this meeting. That was a momentous discovery – getting people on a task larger than their own agendas helps them find common ground.

A Global Context and Self-Management

Emery and Trist also adapted open systems thinking, building on the ideas of biologist Ludwig von Bertalanffy (1952), the creator of "general systems theory." His core concept – that everything in nature connects with everything else – fit neatly with Asch's ideas that we all live on the same planet and share a common psychology.

BION AND SELF-MANAGEMENT

The psychiatrist Wilfred Bion's group dynamics constitute a key building block in Search Conference history. Bion and Trist had a long association, starting in World War II, when they used leaderless groups to select British Army officers. Successful candidates had to walk the tightrope between personal survival and group welfare — exactly the battlefield dilemma. So powerful was this process, it became a core practice of training groups in the post-war Tavistock Institute of Human Relations. When we invite people to self-manage their tasks in future search conferences, we are building on Trist's and Bion's work (Bion, 1961). Our own "self-manager" guide, an invitation for people to share meeting leadership, recording, reporting, and time-keeping stems directly from the leadership studies.

Working with Trist, Emery (1978) also identified "the second design principle" – unspecialized teamwork and shared coordination and control rather than fragmented responsibilities. (The first design principle, sometimes called "Taylorism" after the inventor of scientific management, locates coordination and control outside the work group). Sharing control and coordination helps us manage what Emery and Trist (1964) called "turbulent environments." In a future search, the most dramatic example of this principle is when 60 or more people identify common future themes together, first in one group, then in pairs of groups, finally as a whole conference.

From Emery and Trist we derived the importance of a global context, a whole systems perspective, and people taking responsibility for their own planning. Emery integrated Asch and von Bertalanffy, building four kinds of explorations into his conference model:

- the relations among external environmental factors "outside" the boundaries of the search focus;
- relations within the boundaries of the focal system;
- the impact of the external environment on the system;
- the system's potential to influence its environment.

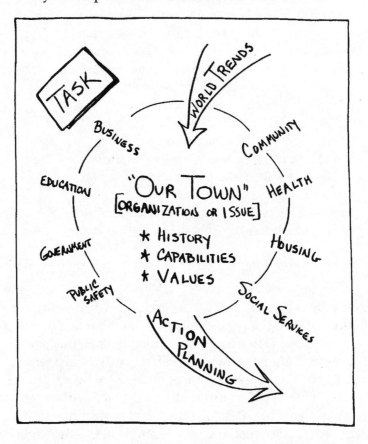

The translation in a future search is straightforward. We put our task in the middle, e.g. "The Future of Our Town." We indicate we are going to look at the trends in society swirling around Our Town, the interactions among Our Town residents, their history and aspirations, the impact of external trends on the community, and how action planning within Our Town can impact the world beyond. To improve the "whole system" means to take all these relationships into account.

Dynamic Map: The 4-Room Apartment

In addition to group composition and tasks, our conference embodies a set of dynamic interactions that occur when a diverse group of people explore their past, present, and future. How can we conceptualize the nature of the process we are managing?

One vivid metaphor for the dynamic experience of change that we like very much is Swedish social psychologist Claes Janssen's (1982) "4-room apartment." This concept has influenced organizational change practices widely in North America and Scandinavia. The idea is simple, easy to talk about, and connects with peoples' everyday experience. We present it at the start of each future search. It can serve as an explicit road map, marking a sometimes difficult route for participants and facilitators. It describes how people might behave at different points in the conference. Using it, we legitimize denial and confusion.

In "contentment" we accept things the way they are, making the best of what is, without hassling. What moves us out of contentment is an unfamiliar experience that disturbs the status quo. We'd rather not admit, let alone deal with, what has happened. So we go into the "denial" room, where we act as if everything's okay when at a deep level an unheard little voice nags us that things are a mess. At some point, however, we are likely to own up. When we admit we are frustrated and unsure of what to do, we've gone through the door to "confusion." The decor of the confusion room is high anxiety. We are in the mess and know it. Only then are we ready for new opportunities.

In future search conferences we do our most creative work in the confusion room. Here we spend roughly half the conference, although it sometimes seems like a lifetime. It is here that we ride the roller-coaster to the emotional depths and heights. Inevitably, people move toward "renewal" as they generate ideal future scenarios. When they identify a common future and start action planning, renewal becomes an unexpected and welcome possibility.

Chapter 4

ROAD MAPS:
THEORY INTO
PRACTICE

"You're unsure when you first come in. You don't know what to expect. And then you get the feeling of. . . it's amazement. Everybody has the same feelings. You begin to feel enthusiasm and challenge."

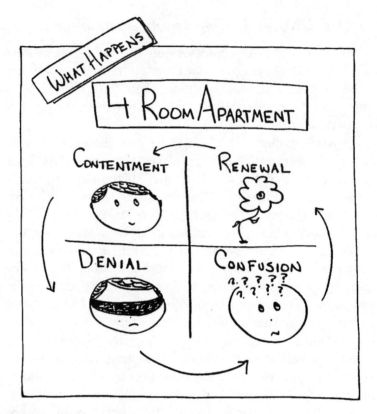

Moving Through the Rooms

We know that many people dislike anxious moments spent facing the complexity of a shared world. It's not worth the effort if we can't do something about it. And alone we can do very little. Understanding how we move through all four rooms together in our conference helps us accept feelings of anxiety, fear, and powerlessness, without which we could not know certainty, security, and empowerment. In future search we validate all feelings. The passage to *renewal* leads from *denial* through *confusion*. We can't get there by any other route. And the roller-coaster, in our metaphor, is the only means of transportation.

In a future search conference, we allow this process. We don't create the rooms or force a group to live in them. We do not try to "make" anything happen. We acknowledge every-

thing that does happen as real, appropriate, and useful for our purposes. In short, we seek to own up to and accept our feelings, not to deny or gloss over them. The highs and lows are a distillation of what we actually experience in a world of constraints and opportunities. Because we move so quickly in such a short time frame, we remember the experience more vividly.

Current Reality and Chaos

We have integrated many other ideas as well. One important source is the work on creativity of Robert Fritz (1989). Fritz showed us how to consider *all* perceptions, past and present, as "current reality." And he persuaded us that holding this reality in our minds as we concretely imagine an ideal future is the surest way to find what we want. Indeed, this path is more certain than structured problem-solving. The impulse to close the gap between current reality and ideal future comes from the tension we experience between the two, and *not* from the specifics of our future "vision." Our unconscious continues to work toward what we want even when we are doing other things. Vision alone won't do it, any more than problem-solving will. We believe a major reason for the degree of implementation that comes from brief future searches is that we hold the tension in awareness as we plan for the future.

We also value Margaret Wheatley's (1992) adaptation of "chaos theory," based in theoretical physics, to an organizational context. Wheatley's insights strengthened our resolve to explore more fully complexity, messiness, confusion, and contradictory information. For some years, we had observed that staying in the confusion room a little longer than people really want to, led to breakthroughs. But until Wheatley's book, we did not understand how apparent disorder functions in nature. The drive to "self-organize" complexity and uncertainty is fundamental to our psyches. We *must* try to make order and meaning of our world, and, given a chance, we will do it.

Having somebody do it for us deprives us of the experience of muddling through to clarity together. We achieve order not by forcing it, but by living with the unknown until we discern a pattern. Many meeting and planning techniques function the opposite way – to simplify complexity, control outcomes, converge data, and impose certainty instead of experiencing the whole mess.

INVOLVING THE WHOLE PERSON

If we have a cutting edge in future search, we believe this is it: to involve ourselves fully in our world and work – head and heart, mind and body, feelings and dreams. Historically, we have experienced a split between cognitive work and creative work that is perpetuated by "task-focused" strategic planning methods. Anything that smacks of fantasy, movement, or non-verbal activity, is thought to be antithetical to serious work on budgets, plans, and programs. Usually "right-brain" activity is relegated to personal growth, creative problem-solving, outdoor leadership training events, and so on.

Many folks find creative processes messy and awkward in performing everyday tasks. Yet we long to bring to our daily work as much capability and creativity as we can muster. Most of it lies unconscious, not necessarily unused, but out of awareness and less accessible. We have come to expect a split between learning and doing in public life. Therefore, it's not easy to bring non-linear processes to bear where people would benefit the most from them without introducing some form of "training." We believe these processes form a "missing link" between good ideas and their execution. As we learn to make this linkage in task-focused meetings we will see faster implementation of anything we want to do.

Many people now are choosing the road toward more fully using everything they have in everything they do. Theoretical and practical sources for mind/body wholeness make up a big section of bookstores and libraries. In five

"I was frustrated, ready to move forward, wanting to do something. When we finally got there, I recognized we had to go through that before we were ready to sit down and do what we were going to do."

minutes we came up with many examples that have strongly affected us, starting with Korzybski's *Science and Sanity* (1948), Jung's famous essays on psychology (1966) and including Berman's *Coming to Our Senses* (1990), Sheldrake's *The Presence of the Past* (1988) and Wilber's *No Boundary* (1985).

Mind/Body Integration in Future Search

However, our intent in this chapter is to identify concepts we have used explicitly in designing a future search. For us, the most direct experience with mind/body connections has come through John and Joyce Weir, a psychologist and dance therapist respectively, who have had an incalculable impact on thousands of people, and whose work is largely unknown because it is largely undocumented. Marv has had the good fortune to co-lead a workshop with John Weir (1971) over many years, and both of us helped produce a video on the Weirs' learning laboratory in "self-differentiation" (Merrill, 1991).

From the Weirs we have learned that we can't force change on ourselves; that keeping aware and moving around (literally) helps us contact our own buried wishes, hopes, fears, and experiences, and that we are self-defeating when we rush ourselves through the confusion room. We also have learned that everybody is doing the best they can with what they have.

We also want to acknowledge the origin in the work of psychologist Yvonne Agazarian (1993) of our understanding of how people face critical forks in the road – between experiencing fully or retreating to more familiar explanations as a substitute for experience. There are many points in a future search where we might be tempted to do the latter – facing a mind-map, acknowledging disagreements, rationalizing common themes. Agazarian's teaching, like the Weirs, is to stay in the moment and describe your experience, don't explain it.

Learning from these colleagues who work in a realm quite different from future search, has enriched our practice on

many levels not obvious from a bare bones description of our design. We have learned how easy it is to separate ourselves from impulses we don't like and to blame others for our troubles. We have learned that we act according to our perceptions of the world and other people, not according to what is right, true, good, or necessary.

We have become especially sensitized to the differing ways we all experience the same events. We have come to know that we have all the parts in us – good, bad, ridiculous, sublime, smart, dumb, arrogant, humble, bigoted, open-minded, sweet-tempered, ill-natured, cynical, and idealistic. Above all, we have learned that the fastest way to help ourselves change is to fully experience, accept, and take responsibility for our thoughts, actions, feelings, and desires.

We manage a future search mindful of these understandings. We give ourselves the courage to let people say whatever they are going to say and groups do whatever they are going to do without correcting participants or blaming ourselves or others for anything that comes up. As a result, we find ourselves more accepting of whatever happens in future searches as the only thing that could have happened.

Asch says the world is governed by "lawful processes" that are knowable only when people listen to each other. We believe the ultimate "lawful process" is that what is, is, whether we can make sense of our experience or not. We can only work with what participants are willing to bring to the table. This understanding we take to be central to a future search.

Finally, underlying all our work is a set of assumptions about how we learn. The list below is taken, almost unchanged, from a workshop handout developed 20 years ago. Our experiences in future search to date validate these assumptions.

LEARNING ASSUMPTIONS (WEISBORD, 1975)

We assume that each person:

1. Has a unique learning style. Some learn best by reading, others by doing, still others by discussing or listening. Hence, we provide a variety of methods, not all of which will suit everyone.

2. Learns at a different rate. Hence some may be confused or "lost" in early stages. It's okay not to "get it" the first time you hear it. Try to be patient with yourself and others.

3. Learns different things from a common experience. Hence we encourage trading of perceptions and acceptance of different feelings and views.

4. Learns best from his or her own experience. Hence we urge testing ideas against your own situation and support a healthy skepticism towards the "one best way."

5. Learns more in one conference than the world will permit us to apply. Hence we focus on local action within a global context.

6. Has the ability to help and teach others. Hence we encourage participation and drawing on each others' expertise as well as ours.

7. Benefits from trial, error, and feedback, if given support and a chance for success. Hence we provide opportunities for this to happen in relatively low-risk situations. No one is required to invest in these opportunities.

CHAPTER 5

Developing a Future Search Design

> "Experts can explain anything in the objective world to us, yet we understand our own lives less and less. In short, we live in the post modern world where everything is possible and almost nothing is certain....The artificial world order of the past has collapsed and a new, more just order has not yet emerged. The central political task of the final years of this century, then, is the creation of a new model of coexistence among the various cultures, peoples, races and religious spheres within a single interconnected civilization."
>
> – Vaclav Havel

ALL FACILITATORS go through a process of trial and error to get meeting designs they can depend on. We believe we can save folks considerable thrashing around if they understand the evolution of future search. The design originated in 1982 out of diverse experiments to develop new models for collaboration in organizations. In the last decade we have experimented with every aspect of the design in many other settings.

Updating Designs

What follows is a detailed account of the development of the future search model. By the time you read this we will

have tried other wrinkles, but we do not intend to change our key conditions for success until we have better ones. Future search is not an answer to every tactical and strategic change dilemma, only a promising direction for new ways of working when the old ways don't work so well. So we are always open to further experimentation with our design.

We work toward design ideas that:

- Enable folks to do a task more simply with the same or better output;
- More fully embody self-management and personal responsibility;
- Enable a fuller confrontation of complexity in the same or less time by more people;
- Further dialogue and the hearing of everybody by everybody in the time available;
- Enhance the ability to have all tasks worked publicly by everyone;
- Place coordination/control of future search tasks more fully in participant hands;
- Engage the whole person, body and mind together.

We steer clear of changes that:

- Reduce group experiences to individual activities;
- Reduce the need for dialogue and open expression;
- Mechanically converge data, set priorities, or categorize issues;
- Take people away from encountering each others' feelings and dreams;
- Deprive a group of the chance to control its own work;
- Add complex steps or instructions to simple tasks.

Some of these ambitions may be contradictory. For example, to fully turn over control to participants is to have no design at all. Managing the time strictly, an unavoidable need in future search, results in some people being shut down just

as they are warming to a task. And there is a fine line between tasks that enable and tasks that control. Moreover, behind our values statements is an assumption – that making certain design changes will enable more open systems capable of self-regulation. We don't imagine we will ever live up to this aspiration as fully as we would like – but it does suggest what concerns us.

Everything Works, Everything Fails

We want to make two important points at the start. *Every* variation on the future search method has worked, even some with obvious flaws. (Many folks have run good conferences using the brief outline from *Productive Workplaces*.) We should also point out that every variation has failed – when used with the wrong group, or on too vague a task, or shortened to the point where people do not work through the sticky parts together, or where so much of the event is controlled that participants feel like puppets rather than partners. Indeed, we don't use the term "future search" to describe such meetings, though we are aware that others do.

A coherent set of design principles helps us navigate the rapids. We did not start with a coherent set. We derived our principles over many years. What follows is a task-by-task account of our ideal conference and how we hit upon this particular integration after some anxious-making learning.

We have integrated our road maps (Chapter 4) into an experience that reflects all of them, but does not find the answer in any of them. We do not believe any single theory encompasses the whole of reality. Nor that any one aspect of future search alone guarantees a successful event. What follows is a detailed run-down on the way we do it. Our focus here is on the dynamic experience both in managing and participating in conferences.

DAY ONE

START-UP

The event starts between 1:00 p.m. and 5:00 p.m. In the early days, we would often start with a 2 1/2 hour review of the past. We soon learned that many people lose their sense of purpose if we end Day 1 still in the past. Now we schedule 4 1/2 hours on the first day. This allows us to review the past and move into the present. So we have a sense of movement that satisfies most people. At the same time, by moving into portraying the present before we sleep, more people are confused or overwhelmed by the end of the day. This is not a bad thing.

Anxiety and confusion will quickly turn to energy next morning. We have learned that people experience more rapid shifts in head, heart, and psyche by adding a few hours. Now we strongly urge our sponsors to schedule a long half-day on Day 1, no matter what the starting time.

OPENING SESSION

People always sit in *mixed* groups to start. In one early conference participants were seated in stakeholder groups at the start. We discovered that sitting with folks who have similar issues makes it harder for people to get into a universal frame of mind. They tend to recycle old information and the dynamics of existing relationships. In mixed groups, people have no history to undo, but probably bring stereotypes and projections. Because of the nature of this meeting, folks are less likely to act these out.

So now we start *only* in mixed groups. In all their diversity people confront the wider world – and themselves – instead of confronting each other. This enables a subtle perceptual shift that allows us to experience others in less judgmental ways. It is harder to achieve new perceptions in confrontation or problem-solving. Looking outward together is one way of opening the door to community-building without making it a "have-to."

We want to establish at the outset that this is a unique planning conference, in that the focus is participant interaction, not leadership from the podium. (We avoid podiums.) A sponsor or steering committee member welcomes people and tells why the conference matters to them personally and how it could benefit participants.

The Past

REVIEW OF THE PAST

The first task establishes personal histories, key world events and milestones in the life of "X" (our future search focus). Having first made notes alone, people transfer their items to butcher paper on the wall. Within 45 minutes everyone is on their feet writing up their own experiences. We learn very quickly that (a) all views are valued, and (b) everybody owns the markers and flip charts. Moreover, it's okay to get up and move around, and our conference can tolerate a lot of hustle and bustle.

Yet, the flip-charting for this task bothered us for a long time. For years we had people post their items on vertical flip charts, hung in three places under headings of "World," "Self" and "X." We had groups report detailed stories, each rich and interesting, based on their reading of one set of charts. What was missing was an integrated picture – how each set of events was related to the others. We would discuss this in the large group, sometimes eliciting startling insights. Sometimes groups just recycled what was already said. We also were uneasy that different groups worked with global, personal and local histories *without* the facility to take an integrated look.

"THE PAST IS PRELUDE"

In 1993 we made a simple technological breakthrough that has had a profound impact on the way a group experiences its own history. We discovered that 4 feet x 8 feet Foamcore wall boards free us from wall-space limitations (see Chapter

11). Now we create three time lines that are taped separately on the walls so people can easily write on them. They are re-taped in parallel on one 8 x 24 feet wall prior to small group discussions. Now *everybody* can make connections among our personal and global pasts and the fate of "X." We ask each group to look through the lens of one time line, global, personal, or local, to tell us a story and note how it relates to the other lines. We cannot imagine a faster way to satisfy the first two of Asch's criteria for effective dialogue – experiencing that we all live on the same planet and are psychologically the same – than by having everybody face the whole.

There is one drawback. All have to find space in front of the same wall, a problem that grows with the size of the group. We do *not* seek to solve this problem for groups. This is a moment when people have a chance to take responsibility for organizing their own work, a key principle of self-management. After some initial milling around, every group solves the problem. Some take notes and go to a corner or back to their table. Some sit on the floor in front of the wall. Some move their chart closer and have a stand-up meeting. This level of group problem-solving furthers our purposes. People discover they can work a complex task simply, despite the apparent messiness.

Simplifying Worksheets

We have had to resist the temptation to add more and more "good" questions to worksheets, to elaborate the tasks, point people in more directions, and shape their experience. We see no benefit in detailed instructions, other than the relief of consultant anxiety. If anything, the more sub-parts to a task, the harder it is to do. Moreover, we may distract a group from the issues *it* believes are relevant. A couple of simple, open-ended questions are sufficient to satisfy both the information-sharing and community-building purposes of a future search. All elaboration seems to us now to be self-defeating. We were not born knowing this. We learned by trial and error. Notice how 10 complex questions in 1990 became 3 simple questions in 1994.

HOW A WORKSHEET BECAME SIMPLER

1990 Example
Search Task: FUTURE OF SERVICES IN CORPORATION"X"
Worksheet Assignments

Table 1 – Analyze OUR PERSONAL EXPERIENCE
　　　　across all eras.
1. How would you characterize the experience, backgrounds, skills of people here?
2. How are we similar, how different?
3. What is our potential as a group in this context?

Table 2, 3, 4 – Analyze the HISTORY OF OUR FIELD
　　　　across all eras.
1. What milestones and critical changes do you identify?
2. How would you characterize the development of this industry over the last 30 years?
3. Given our past, what would you consider an ideal future for this field in the next decade – the one you would most like to see come about?

Tables 5, 6 – CORPORATION X'S MILESTONES
1. Characterize the company's development across 30 years in a few sentences.
2. What stands out for you?
3. What do you believe is the most desirable future for the conference entity over the next decade?

Tables 7, 8 – THE WORLD
– Draw a line down the middle of a flip chart. On one side, (1) Characterize changes of the last 30 years. What stands out for you? On the other side, note your IDEAL FUTURE for this planet over the next decade. What would you really like to have/make happen.

1994 Example
Search Task: FUTURE OF HOUSING IN SANTA CRUZ
COUNTY
Worksheet Assignments

1. Table(s)_____
a. Use the Personal time line to tell us a story about
the people in this room.
b. Look at the Personal time line in relationship to the
other two. What patterns do you see?

2. Table(s)_____
a. Use the Global time line to tell us a story about our
recent world history.
b. Look at the Global time line in relationship to the
other two. What patterns do you see?

3. Table(s)_____
a Use the Santa Cruz County time line to tell us a
story of our community history.
b. Look at the Santa Cruz County time line in relation-
ship to the other two. What patterns do you see?

Now, mixed groups develop a picture of where we have been and how we got here. This process is repeated in each task – everyone supplies information and helps interpret what they hear. Each group reports its conclusions. Then we have a whole group dialogue on what we've noticed and learned.

The Present

FOCUS ON PRESENT: EXTERNAL TRENDS AFFECTING "X"

Next, the conference reorganizes into stakeholder groups. People take a minute to present a news clip they brought and tell why they consider it important here. This has the effect of

Planning a Future Search

⇧ *Defining the Task:*
 Why Do This Now?

"We chose a very difficult topic for this community. Who's problem is housing really? Is it just the people who can't afford it or is it all of us? By looking at housing in a broader context and by involving more people in the issue we moved it out of the political domain to the domain of the community."

⇧ *Selecting*
 Stakeholders

"We decided we wanted educators, people from churches, all kinds of non-profits, farm workers, business, government, students, retirees…"

⇦ "We're growing so dramatically in the corporation it's scary and exciting. Can we have some sort of control and direction? I think a lot of people will be excited about a process where they might have a say in what happens in the growth."

⇧ "We couldn't fall back on any of our old tools. We had to sit there and practice what we hoped to implement in the future search. Every voice is valid. We can't impose our stereotypes. We can't assume that we know the best way."

Getting Started

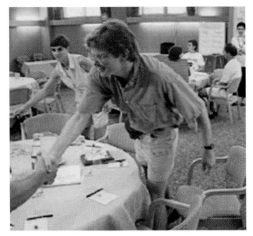

"To regain our position as a manufacturing leader and compete in a worldwide recessive economy, we must be willing to change."

⇧ "I came into the room and thought, well, if nothing else comes out of this, this is the most diverse party anybody's ever given."

"Expect to hang out in confusion. It's a jigsaw puzzle with pieces that may feel overwhelming. The road to renewal often leads through denial and confusion."

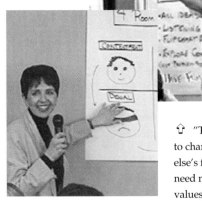

⇧ "There's no need for anybody to change their mind or anybody else's for us to be successful. You need not give up your beliefs, values, and commitments."

⇨ "I'm with the Beach Community Project. Here's a picture by a boy who went to prison and now wants to be a community leader."

⇧ "Here is an eggshell broken into pieces and painted with many colors. The pieces are scattered, however interdependent, moving in a kind of wave towards this egg which is a whole."

Recalling the Past

⇧ *Creating Global, Personal, and Local Time Lines*

⇩ "Pre-1968, we went from hope to shock; from 1969–75 we saw heightened mistrust and confusion, and a growing sense of self-reliance. Since 1984 we have a sense of confusion, insecurity with growing violence and a sense of helplessness. At the same time we see a need to heal, and refocus on community."

⇧ *Noting Milestones*

"A lot of people were left out of the post-World War II group—so we start the women's movement, the civil rights movement, the war on poverty. Technology affected our lives. We're now a global community. We're affected by AIDS and gang violence."

⇧ *Making History Visible, Discovering Patterns, Telling Stories about What the Past Means*

Appreciating the Present

⇧ *Describing Trends*

"I contributed things I thought everybody knew. The response was, 'Oh, really?' The map helped everyone see their community through other eyes."

⇧ *Recording Trends
and Concerns*

"It gives you an appreciation for the complexity. You realize you can't handle everything."

⇩ "The confusion is: How can we put this all together and come out with something positive?"

⇦ *Touching
"The
Mess"—
Noting
Trends*

"The sense of community was destroyed so long ago that a lot of us have forgotten what it's like to know the person next door. We're all burning out."

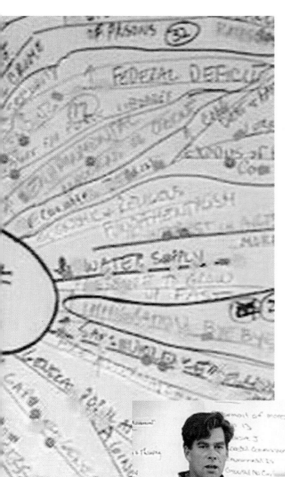

"We looked at lack of youth and family opportunities, declining jobs, and loss of community. We have gang and intervention programs and threats of punishment; we want new education structures, more vocational education, extra classes after school; mentor programs."—*Health and Education stakeholder group*

⇧ *Owning What We Do Now*

"We're proud of our ethnic and religious diversity. We're sorry we don't have enough help for youths in the streets."—*Community Activists stakeholder group*

"We're sorry we are in our own individualistic way working in isolation. We're proud that we are becoming more part of the change process… not as resistant as we were."—*Business stakeholder group*

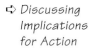

⇨ *Discussing Implications for Action*

Living the Future

Present-
ing as
if the
Dream
Has
Come
True

⇧ Developing Ideal Scenarios

⇧ "We've worked out an on-the-job training program with the school system. We're attracting tourists. We've preserved our tall trees. We have a recycling industry creating jobs."

⇧ "We have a cultural center for agriculture and a regional market."

"We have adopted a declaration of interdependence: We hold these truths to be self-evident, that all species are necessary parts of the human mosaic of life. Every person has value, the right to be treated with dignity and respect, the right to a safe and healthy environment."

Confirming Common Ground and Potential Projects

Identifying Common Themes

Reality Dialogue: What Are We Really Agreeing to Do?

"I look at things in a practical everyday world. We do things according to density, that's how we build. Am I the only one who thinks like that? I'd like to hear if anybody else agrees with me."

Merging Themes with Other Groups

"We need to look at preservation of farmland and the environment in relation to housing. Housing sometimes comes into conflict with both."

Posting and Grouping Themes

"I'm willing to work for certain types of projects, not just any local housing project. I think there is some disagreement. That's fine with me."

⇦ "I see an equality/diversity theme, government, neighborhoods, business partnerships, safe environment, and mass transit as themes supported by the whole conference."

Moving Into Action

"We came up with concrete short-range goals. The first is to make sure we reach low-income people on home-ownership opportunities. We need volunteers from banking and real estate to help with the research."

⇧ *Making Long- and Short-Range Plans*

⇨ *Taking Respon-sibility for Action*

"We are going to develop a network of stakeholders on employment and education with emphasis on including the Latino community."

"We are going to begin work on a cultural arts center for the valley."

"Our chief of police is going to make a presentation to council, stressing the importance of the work we've done here on the issue of housing."

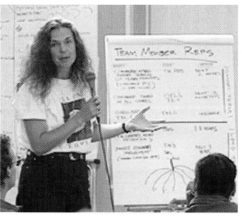

"This wasn't just two days spent talking and sharing. People were going to take action and continue the conference in their own small communities. I really felt good."

⇦ *Making Public Commit-ments*

"pump-priming" for the next task. When we started working with "futurizing" in the early 1980's, we used John Naisbitt's "Megatrends" (1982). We asked people to generate their own trends, then compare them with the expert's. Lo and behold, the trends people listed were 85 percent congruent with Naisbitt's, which is not surprising, for his trends came from content analyses of newspapers.

NAISBITT'S MEGATRENDS AS OF 1982

1. Industrial Society toward Information Society
2. Forced Technology toward High Tech/High Touch
3. National Economy toward World Economy
4. Short term toward Long Term
5. Centralization toward Decentralization
6. Institutional Help toward Self-Help
7. Representative Democracy toward Participatory Democracy
8. Hierarchies toward Networking
9. North toward South
10. Either/Or toward Multiple Option

So we cut out the middle-person, asking people to bring their own news articles. This got folks invested in the meeting beforehand. Still, the task in this form left us with long lists on flip charts, good lists to be sure, but awfully linear. In the mid-80's we adapted Tony Buzan's (1976) creative "mind map" methodology. We believe that making a mind map and going toward it (when the natural impulse is to recoil) promotes ownership of the "mess" – our contradictory, confusing, fast-shifting, present reality. This device has proved especially powerful in helping a group make visible a broad pattern of concerns rarely faced in any setting where people can act together. (A typical mind-map enlivens the center section of this book.)

Buzan's practical groundrules for group mind maps have made an unthinkable logistical feat doable in an hour or less.

By asking every person to say where on the map to put his or her item, and what words to use, we avoid interpreting, controlling, or shaping people's thoughts. More, we get richer information as folks call out their items, build on each other's connections, and give us examples of what they mean.

MAKING A MIND MAP

First, we invite everybody to "come on down" to the wall designated for this purpose. We want folks close in. The conference task is written in the center of a sheet of butcher paper 6 feet high by 12 feet wide. We want to map all the external trends that are having an impact on our conference topic now. We mind map as a total group so everybody hears what matters to others. This is an interactive community experience. Ideas and connections trigger other ideas and connections.

"The mind map not only describes your own community, but also you begin to see all the global and national forces that have a bearing on everybody's communities."

We want everybody to hear everybody else, so we take one trend at a time, writing as quickly as possible. We ask for a trend. When we get a response, e.g. "Increased environmental awareness," we draw a line out from the circle and write those words on the line. We usually ask for an example, and get "More recycling." We consider concrete examples very important if we are to understand what is going through a speakers' minds when they add a trend. Whenever feasible, we add the person's example to the map.

Then we ask for another trend. Somebody calls out "increasing health care costs." We ask, "Is that a new issue or does it branch off of something already there?" If new, we draw a new line from the center in a different color. As speakers connect their issues to those already on the map, we draw each cluster of related issues in its own color. If people flag opposing trends, both increasing and decreasing medical costs, for instance, we put both perceptions up, always asking for concrete examples. They are looking at different parts of the same elephant.

```
┌─────────────────────────────────┐
│  ┌──────────────────┐           │
│  │ MIND MAP         │           │
│  └──────────────────┘           │
│                                 │
│  • ALL IDEAS ARE VALID          │
│                                 │
│  • PEASON WHO NAMES ISSUE       │
│      SAYS WHERE IT GOES          │
│                                 │
│  • OPPOSING TRENDS ARE O.K.      │
│                                 │
│  • GIVE CONCRETE EXAMPLES        │
│                                 │
└─────────────────────────────────┘
```

Validating Every Person's Reality

Sometimes people have a hard time putting their issue into words. Usually, a person who fumbles without "getting to the point" has something particularly important that would help the group. The same condition holds when a participant isn't sure where the issue goes on the map. We make it a practice to stay with the person until he/she decides. Often, group tension rises and there may be pressure to keep moving. We are *not* seeking time efficiency here. We wish to validate every person's reality.

We believe that there is great value in making psychological boundaries easier to cross – especially the boundary between what's inside our heads and what we say in public. We want to get through the embarrassment, shyness or negative thoughts like "my contribution isn't that important." There is always energy behind the barriers that people put up for themselves. Every person who volunteers an item

OTHER WAYS OF USING MIND MAPS

Many people want the mind map to be something more familiar. They ask for statistical validity, they want priority voting, they want to "improve" the process by a forced ranking of the issues. All of this is a *different* kind of activity that contradicts the aims of a future search. The purpose of a group mind map is to immerse ourselves in our collective concerns, face the confusion and provide a basis for dialogue. The map does not require statistical validity for a conference to get the desired results.

Other folks like to start off with categories, so that the branches will be neater. For example, a "health care" branch, and an "environment" branch, and a "globalization" branch, etc. We like it messy just the way it pops out of people's brains. We want to live with the anxiety that goes with keeping stuff open, and not falsify order to soften our encounter with ambiguity. This is an exercise in systems behavior, not expert systems thinking. That is, we discover how systems self-organize when they slog through for themselves and create patterns that have *not* been provided by consultants or facilitators. However, it does leave us open to charges that we are not making things clear the way folks expect facilitators to do.

is worth our time. Sometimes a person will ask to think about it a while, and then come back with a gem that illuminates us. No contribution, however off-beat or obscure, is ever irrelevant.

Many people are not used to thinking descriptively. When we hear solutions instead of trends, we ask, "What trend is that a solution to?" If we hear problems, we ask what trend that problem reflects. We persist, but every map is a mishmash of trends, problems, solutions, and concerns. This has

no discernible effect on the outcome of a conference, although it may violate a facilitator's sense of what people "should" be doing at this stage. So we also keep reminding ourselves that no matter what we ask for, people say what is on the tips of their tongues.

It is particularly difficult in conferences sponsored by a single organization to get people to stay with the impact of "external" trends on their organizations. Nearly always, a number of folks are more invested in the impact of organizational policies, norms, and practices on *them*. Inevitably this information comes out. We accept what we hear, we restate that we seek a collective portrait of world and societal trends, and ask for a connection between the problem and the underlying trend.

No Two Maps Are Alike

Whatever people put on the map is what's on their minds as they contemplate their situation with others who can help or hurt. The map is *their* map, the good, the bad, and the ugly. Folks often express awe (fear mixed with wonder) at the complexity. Sometimes this takes the form of stunned silence. Sometimes it takes the form of looking for somebody to blame for "distracting us" with so many issues. We believe the map is a pretty good visualization of Jung's "collective unconscious" in this group in this place.

Often folks comment on how much negative stuff is up there. Sometimes this leads to a rash of positive trends, sometimes to a search for reasons. We believe the strong feelings building up in a group at this point are natural, inevitable, and functional if the future search is to succeed. We have learned not to do anything to take away the anxiety, pain, or confusion, but to live with it – in ourselves and in the conference.

Eventually the exercise winds down with a few folks still having items to put in and most of the group fidgeting and ready to quit for the day. That is a very good place to stop. We have never done less than 30 minutes of mind-mapping, and sometimes have gone for an hour. About 45 minutes is

Chapter 5

DEVELOPING
A FUTURE
SEARCH
DESIGN

"One key thing was people's willingness to admit to their confusion. Right from the beginning, the group that was most interested in getting involved were those who said, 'I don't known how to solve the affordable housing problem.'"

average. We ask people to reflect on where they are at the moment, and how they experience what we have done. We consider this task a pivot point of our conference, usually the low point on our roller-coaster. The map becomes a potent symbol of our common world. Collectively we are aware of nearly everything.

Moving Toward the "Mess"

We have one more task before the evening break. Each person has a strip of seven sticky dots, color matched by stakeholder group. They are asked to place the dots on the trends they consider most important for the conference. They may put all seven on one trend, four on one and three on another, or on seven different trends, for example. This is not a poll to set priorities, but rather visual data for the dialogue that will take place next morning. The colors also show quickly which groups care about what trends.

This simple task has important consequences. First, every person has to read all the trends and consider how they are related. Second, they must move toward the "mess" when their tendency might be to retreat to the bar for a drink. Third, they actually touch the map when they affix their dots, claiming ownership for the trends that matter to them. Before dinner on Day 1 every person has joined in producing a collective reality rarely encountered in a public meeting.

Keeping Everything Public

Most important, this is a sobering experience. We have created this world together and we now face it together, listening to each other, building on each other's perceptions. We believe mind-mapping in a future search should not be done as a silent "affinity diagram" or with computer inputs and voting. Methods that reduce anxiety and make the task easier to bear (or facilitate) may blunt the shared experience.

Confusion, chaos, and contradictions are inherent in a group's varied perceptions. *We do not wish to reconcile these perceptions through agreement OR avoidance.* We want them

acknowledged as paradox and confusion. We want to make it harder for people to hold to the fantasy that "we" are clear on the situation, and "they" are confused, or vice versa. The truth is that none of us has *the* truth. To the extent that we face this fact, we will develop more effective organizations and more livable communities.

THE ZEIGARNICK EFFECT

When we end the day in the middle of a task, the need remains in us to complete unfinished business. This insight was proven by Bluma Zeigarnick, a student of Kurt Lewin's at Berlin University in the 1920's. Lewin, a genius at building theory from everyday events, noticed how a waiter in his favorite coffee shop kept a running total in his head, no matter how large the group, what they ate, or how long they sat. Once the bill was paid he promptly forgot the bill. Zeigarnick, in a series of experiments, showed that we build up a store of energy that is discharged by completing a task (Weisbord, 1987, p. 86). By breaking in the middle both evenings of a future search, we keep learning alive in the group and make start up each morning easy.

DAY TWO

FOCUS ON PRESENT – LOOKING AT TRENDS

The next morning, before working with the mind map, we like to highlight those trends with the most dots on them. One way to do this is to circle those connected branches that have a significant number of dots, usually with six or eight clusters of issues. These can be listed on a flip chart together with the number of dots they attracted. We like to involve participants in managing this step. We neither add nor subtract issues, nor change the language people have used. The clusters reflect connections made in the group. Drawing circles around

clusters is the closest we ever come to sorting information for a conference. And indeed, this step can be done by participants, or skipped.

We *always* discuss what we see (collectively) before moving on to small group tasks. We like to have the whole group stand in front of the map, just as they did when we made it, and consider the various clusters of issues. We report back what we observe on the map, but we don't interpret what it means. We ask participants to contribute their observations as well. This exercise does not lock anybody into anything. After half an hour or so, we are ready to have people re-interpret the map within their stakeholder groups.

Which Group Should Interpret the Mind Map?

What are the consequences of having a mind-map interpreted by stakeholder groups rather than mixed groups? In early conferences we alternated between the two structures for this task. Given our task sequence, we found that people see the whole better when they explore the present in stakeholder groups. They learn two dimensions they cannot learn in mixed groups – what their peers are thinking, and what other stakeholder groups are doing and want to do. When we did this task in mixed groups, we lost a powerful source of reality data that we now know helps people more fully experience their common agenda.

Hearing how others with identifiable stakes see the complexity, and what matters most to them, reduces stereotyping. It also enables the third Asch condition for effective dialogue – owning the facts of each others' worlds. In so doing, people also own their own reality and their stake in the whole. Whatever people say, we believe *that* is our "current reality." Whether we like our issues or don't like them, they are indubitably *ours*.

The mind map worksheet, too, has gotten simpler. Where once we asked for Ron Lippitt's "events, trends, and developments" (ETD's), we now invite trends alone. We cannot

discern any drop off in complexity, richness, or understanding from this simpler instruction.

STAKEHOLDER PERSPECTIVES: THE PRESENT

Stakeholders may choose to discuss any trends they consider important. For some years we asked them to note three or so trends and write on a flip chart what they are doing now and what they want to do in the future. We soon became aware that this activity tended to make people isolate clusters again—a sort of problem list—instead of thinking integratively as they had done while making the map.

So we began trying other procedures. The most successful of these to date is to ask each stakeholder group to make its own version of the mind map, showing the relationship among the trends that they consider most important to them. We also ask them to note on their map what they are doing now and what they *want* to do that they are *not* doing now about trends they consider important.

As each group reports, we hear for the first time the extent to which stakeholders share common or diverse concerns. These observations usually go unspoken in ordinary meetings. People are surprised at which groups care about what, and realize that a lot of us worry about the same issues and want to live in the same kind of world. There is a great deal more helpful stuff going on than any of us realized. What seemed hopeless last night becomes more hopeful this morning.

FOCUS ON THE INTERNAL PRESENT: PROUDS/SORRIES

Next we look at how stakeholder groups feel about what they are doing now vis-a-vis our future search topic. We do this with a task learned from Ron Lippitt and Eva Schindler-Rainman (1980): noting what people are proud of and sorry about in their own work with "X." "Prouds and sorries" has moved in and out of the design several times as we sought to understand its function. One reason is that the sorries list can become a litany of problems. In one conference, folks went into a paroxysm of breast-beating and finger-pointing be-

cause their sorries lists seemed endless. So we dropped the task – and were sorry for, not proud of, our faint hearts. In another conference, we dropped it for fear it would duplicate data reported in the previous task. Again, we were sorry. One organizational development standby we tried was a variation on "start, stop, continue" lists. It's a cognitive rationalization of prouds and sorries. We believe that people "stop, start, and continue" naturally when they dramatize ideal futures.

Two modifications have made a big difference to this task. First, instead of asking for prouds and sorries in general, we ask what each stakeholder group is doing right now in relation to the conference topic that it feels proud of and sorry about. Our slogan is, "Own it, don't moan it." We invite people to hear what others are saying, not to *do* anything. Our perceptions of our own behavior, good news and bad, need to be public for people to get beyond blaming and complaining. The whole purpose is taking responsibility.

"I think we covered every base possible....We didn't leave a stone unturned."

Taking responsibility

We have found group after group shifting their perceptions of themselves and each other in this task. In Asch terms, owning up helps us perceive our equal humanity, vulnerability, and aspiration. For example, team leaders in a team-based plant saying, "Well, we have felt for a long time that people were ducking responsibility, and it's a relief to hear team members put this on their 'sorries' list." Team members heaved a collective sigh hearing leaders say they were sorry they had regressed toward traditional supervision. The mutual "aha" was how each group subtly reinforced the other, *and none of them liked it.* That is a classic spontaneous future search discovery.

As for this exercise duplicating mind-map analyses, we were wrong. The mind-map task is *descriptive* – what we are doing and what we want to do. Prouds/sorries is *affective* – how we feel about what we are doing. In each task we are exploring different aspects of our perceptions, intellectual, and emotional. Both represent what Robert Fritz (1989) calls

"current reality." Each contributes to a central purpose of future search conferences, that is, taking responsibility for ourselves. We can also interpret this step in terms of Claes Janssen's "4-room apartment" (Chapter 4). Making public our prouds and sorries is one way of moving out of the denial room. Since 1988, prouds and sorries has been a fixture of our conferences.

The Future

FOCUS ON THE FUTURE

Our generic design calls for finishing the present, returning to mixed groups, and reviewing the future task before lunch. We give people 2 1/2 hours, including lunch, to prepare their ideal futures. They go back into mixed groups, each containing a cross-section of all stakeholders. We prefer the same groups they started with a day earlier because they can reconnect more quickly and build on earlier learnings. However, a lot has changed for them. Now every person has a deep appreciation of their own and others' stakes in the issues. They have very different ideas about what's feasible than they had 24 hours earlier. Lunch provides useful reconnection time.

In early conferences we experimented with having people produce a portrait of their Ideal versus Probable future. This activity, a feature of Search Conferences based on the Emery/Trist model, is intended to create dissonance between what exists and what people want so that they will move into action. As we worked with mind maps, however, we concluded that the "probable future" usually is expressed as a projection of an even gloomier version of the present. Because we already had an immersion in the world as it is and had built up considerable feelings about living this way, we decided on a different flow of experience.

In our design the dissonance comes from polarizing the present, overwhelmingly gloomy on most mind maps, with what people really want in an ideal future. Meanwhile, we

had grounded ourselves in two relevant insights. One is Ron Lippitt's (1983) insight that people motivate themselves strongly when they act out the future they really want as if it has *already* happened. A second is Robert Fritz's (1989) contention that clear internalized images of the present and future tug the unconscious into seeking ways to close the gap, even without formal action plans.

Acting As If

We can access this dynamic quickly at this point in a future search. We invite mixed groups to put themselves 5,10, or 20 years in the future, imagine that they have made their dreams come true, and list on flips charts (a) concrete images and examples of what has actually happened, and (b) the barriers they had to overcome along the way. Then people are asked present their scenario in any way they choose. We recommend creative presentations – a drama, skit, play, TV news show, etc. People present their scenarios in mid-afternoon. We need at least an hour for eight presentations (e.g. seven minutes each) plus set-up time in between. Before we begin, we ask folks to make notes on themes they hear in other presentations that also occur in their own, and also projects or innovations they like very much.

Creative presentations deeply anchor our hopes and dreams in our bodies and psyches. This is not a trivial point. Doing things which everybody wants that have never been done before requires accessing many levels of capability. This is not simply an emotional or intellectual matter. It is also, as we have learned from the Weirs, a matter of literally *moving*. We think the movement starts in the first hour when people get up and put their experiences on time lines; it accelerates when they go towards the mind map and claim their issues, and is experienced as a real future possibility when they act as if they have made their ideals come true. We believe that folks unable to move in the supportive, energized context of a future search will have a much harder time implementing plans, no matter how compelling they are.

Usually everybody participates rather than having a single

person report for the group, the mode used up until now. We don't require this. It just happens. These scenarios range from highly factual to highly fanciful, depending on the group. Behind every drama, no matter how fanciful, lies a bedrock of reality, grounded in every person's day-to-day experience. We are convinced that acting out our dreams as if we are living them now contributes greatly to widespread implementation. We have dozens of reports of this phenomenon from many sectors. We believe it reflects a practical embodiment of our assumption that the mind and body are one.

However, we believe it's important to lay the groundwork for this event. People may become cynical about free-standing "visioning" that bypasses a sobering trip through current reality. Futuring by itself elicits dreams – but may not generate the commitment to make them come true. The motivation comes when we fully own our present global and local "mess" – the chaos, complexity, and opportunities (or whatever names we put on what in the world is happening to us). At this point in the conference people are mostly likely to ascend to the heights, experiencing being on top of the world. They can't do that if they don't experience the bottom.

CONFIRMING A COMMON FUTURE

We have done more agonizing over the common future task than any other. After all, this is the heart of the matter. How do we arrive at common ground in a way that enables people to take responsibility for their own experience? At the simplest level, we have experimented with language. At first we chose the most obvious label, "consensus futures." We found that "consensus" generally means that a majority prevails after the minority has had its say and agrees to go along. The purpose of future search is to discover what the actuality is, not to make decisions binding on anybody. We have no need to force a convergence. This enables people to make informed choices. They learn what can be done right away, because everybody wants action. So we named the concept "common ground agenda" or "common futures," before settling (for now) on a "common future."

Timing

When we were struggling to do the whole conference in two days we had to identify common themes and make action plans on the afternoon of Day 2. We found that people were overloaded and tired at a critical juncture. More, they had not had a chance to revisit their skepticism, uncertainty, and reluctance to act, which becomes masked by the euphoria of ideal futures. Action planning came at an awkward time, when folks needed to reflect on what they were agreeing to. Moreover, we make more solid commitments when we are fresh and re-charged. We only needed to witness the energy shift a few times before we knew that we wanted to extend our schedule, putting confirmation of the common future and action planning on Day 3.

Documenting Agreements

In early years we let the common future be implicit, not explicit. That is, we did not ask for agreement, only that people hear what others were thinking. The whole group would call out common themes after hearing all reports. We did a variety of things to capture the agreements. In one early conference, pressed for time, we went along with the idea that representatives from each scenario group would meet after the conference and put together a single scenario to be mailed out. That simply delayed a real understanding of the common ground, and slowed down the action planning. We also went the specialist route. Observers watched the ideal scenarios and "fed back" their list of agreed-upon themes for discussion. This led to hassling over "semantics" and nit-picking the observers' categories.

Next, we opted for a representative approach. A volunteer from each group took notes on consensus themes. The volunteers pooled their notes into one list during a break and presented it to the whole. Inevitably they caught a lot of flack for not getting it right, much as the observers had. They ended up feeling misunderstood and abused (they were). Some of our colleagues worked this by having the task force

meet in a fishbowl with an empty chair. This was a slightly better solution. Still, the tension would go up because most people had to sit passively watching. The empty chair became a platform from which to browbeat the task force.

The "aha" had been under our noses for years. We missed it because we had no experience getting 60+ people to self-manage list-building. Yet, that is the challenge. For two days, people had worked together on the same tasks and reported their conclusions. Then, at consensus time we switched gears. Participants resented having their reality boiled down by "specialists" *or* a committee of peers. The solution seems obvious now. Let the whole group tackle the common future too. We will describe the method in a moment.

Naming the Lists

For a time we asked people to compile two lists, "Common Future" and "Potential Future." We wanted to keep good ideas that appeared in some but not all ideal scenarios. The lists became a mix of values and principles on the one hand, and concrete projects, programs, and policies on the other. Often people agreed on values, but not on projects. We stipulated that we were looking for the common future as an umbrella; the potential projects became an inventory of rich ideas and people did not have to agree on them.

If we stayed with only generalities, though, we lost the richness of innovation. More, we avoided confronting what different people meant by values like "environmental responsibility," or "including all views" or "city/suburban cooperation." To deal with this we ran many conferences asking people to put "concrete examples" in parenthesis after each "future" statement. This led to agreement on the main headings, but dissension around some concrete examples.

We learned three key lessons from these dialogues. One, after seeing the world from the depths and heights, people need to revisit their concerns about what they really are agreeing to. It matters not whether their list is made by one person, eight people, or everybody. Two, people still need to clarify, to dissent, and perhaps to nit-pick before they are

willing to commit. We decided it would be a big mistake to design out this opportunity, to gloss it over, or to try to smooth the way with false agreements. (That is what makes people cynical.) Three, we learned that we could be clearer still in what we hoped people would put on their lists. In particular, we could make it simpler to differentiate between what they all wanted and how they might get there.

Self-Managing Towards a Common Future

The method we use now is simple, direct, quick, and people feel satisfied that their reality remains intact. More, it involves everybody in making and confirming the lists, and we time it so that people can sleep on their common ground and unresolved issues before they have to act.

We start the common ground task after the future scenarios on the afternoon of the second day. We ask each scenario group to make three flip charts: One is the "Common Future" framed as *what* we all agree we want. This list tends toward value statements and abstractions. The second list is "Potential Projects" (programs, policies, etc.), concrete proposals for *how* to get what we want. This list captures the many ideas as possibilities, and we need not agree to implement them all. The third list, "Unresolved Differences," recognizes conflicts, major and minor, that have not been worked through yet.

Recently we have experimented with forming new mixed groups, one person from each scenario group, to create these lists. The new group has within it all experiences from all scenario discussions, and can quickly arrive at the whats, hows, and unresolved issues.

When they finish their lists, they pair with another group and merge two sets to one. We ask that the lists be put up on the wall under the three headings. We ask folks to cut the final lists into strips, one issue per strip, so that they can put related items together later. Then we go to dinner.

CONFIRMING A COMMON FUTURE, CONTINUED

Next morning, we invite everybody to gather at the wall and ask participants to group similar themes. They move the strips around until they are satisfied that all related items are together. What are the shared visions and values? How many different ways have we expressed each theme? We see a lot of "stop-start" behavior as people realize this is their last chance for dialogue before they have to act. Anxiety rises again, and some people may become impatient that we don't have closure on all issues. We see this as a step in the right direction, not a set-back near the end. We are no longer dealing in assumptions. We have changed our context and must now reassess what we will do. As the whole group has this dialogue, people are learning what they *actually* are saying to each other.

It is now obvious that the conference facilitators are not going to formulate the issues or action plans. New things will happen *only* if those present choose to make them happen. We read the grouped lists aloud and invite discussion. If things need to be moved or rearranged, people do it. We make sure that the lists reflect what everyone wants. We have no investment in what people agree to or how much of the list remains common ground. We feel successful if people understand what is real for this meeting at this point.

Second Thoughts

No matter what technique we use every group needs up to an hour for total group dialogue. Some people *always* have second thoughts at the point where they have to commit, worrying, for example, about the deep divisions that have not been explored. We check who else has the concern, and discourage the exploration, except to understand the issue. Unresolved differences at this point require much more work than we have time for. If people hang on to an issue, it goes on the "Unresolved" list.

"The list of common futures really reflected some common ground that was heartening for me....These were real people talking about how they live, voices I had not heard, points of view not on the agenda."

We may point out that the group is deciding what can be reported as honest outcomes of this conference. Furthermore, we must decide whether to act now on common ground, which will be easy, or to spend time hassling over unresolved issues. There is not time to do both. Each group must face this turning point.

Recognizing and making the choice is a transformative step. We are not advocating burying conflict or denying the need to keep working out our differences. Nobody is constrained from working their commitments with or without the support of the whole. We simply are pointing out that much misdirected frustration comes from unresolved tensions over things everybody wants to do and nobody has time for. Often, these matters are not trivial. They reflect our highest values and global concerns. Choosing to act on what's possible channels energy that benefits everyone. If people can't do it here and now, they probably can't do it at all.

ACTION PLANNING

Action planning is the task we thought we knew best. Methods have been piling up since the invention of group problem-solving technologies. There are dozens of variations on the theme of giving and getting help, choosing action steps, dividing up the work, deciding what to do next, and creating schedules. We've experimented with many structures for each aspect of this process. In one notable backfire some years ago, we had functional groups send "valentines" to each other proposing actions they desired from others – a prelude to negotiating new relationships. This nearly blew a hard won consensus out of the water, as people embraced a more-familiar paradigm, "I'll do this if you do that."

Also, in corporate conferences, we had people list recommendations for the executive team, whose task it was to talk it over and respond. We have stopped doing this, because it tends to create dependency and "upward delegation." In one meeting people asked the executives to do a long list of things. "You already have the authority to do that!" said the

exasperated CEO. The future search question is, "What are we ready, willing and able to do now *without* negotiation or permission from above?"

Now, we only plan in one mode: People take responsibility for what *they* intend to do. If they need help, they ask for it. They don't buck tough issues up, down, or sideways. You'd be amazed how hard it is for otherwise competent people to catch on to this basic act of self-empowerment. You never know what you can get until you claim it, including authority you didn't know you had.

How Much Time is Needed?

Our minimum design allows three to four hours for two rounds of planning meetings. We have found that this time is adequate for most conferences. If participants live far from each other or can't easily reconnect, they may need more time to build their structure and plan next steps. In that case, we like to add two or three hours, ending at 3:00 p.m. on Day 3. If people have ready access to each other, they may not need as much time.

Keep in mind that this conference is a catalyst for processes that go on for a long time. Often many more people will be involved later. If people are interdependent and want to continue working together, it's wrong to set the expectation that it's now or never. We consider it a big mistake to shorten other key activities in the design to make room for action steps. Our practice is based on years of seeing good flip charts and detailed plans and strategies quickly shelved on Monday morning by people who have solved the problem elegantly and not worked through their own commitment.

Action Planning Groups

Action planning in a future search to us means people deciding next steps, dividing up the work, setting goals, figuring who else to involve, and making public their commitments and timetable. We use simple worksheets (See Appendix B) and, for that reason, some facilitators get nervous and build in more comprehensive methods. There's

nothing wrong with that if participants find such structures useful. We don't think this is a make-or-break issue.

The way to consider action planning techniques is to start with your assumptions about the conditions under which people take responsibility and follow through with their plans. What are the connections between a planning method, the time groups invest, the level of detail they get into, and the degree of implementation? How do people create an umbrella under which they will stay connected for months or years? How do they create a climate and context to gain investment from others *not* at the conference.

It is possible to produce impressive documents from a conference that are made of real ideals, good intentions, and not much else. As consultants, we get a lot of job satisfaction from good conference documentation. But we get even more when we follow up six months or a year later and find people still working on projects born in their future search. How much help do people really need once they figure out what they intend to do?

We would rather respond to requests when people know what they want to do, rather than apply our own assumptions about planning structures and techniques. Every group has different needs. We believe that commitment starts much earlier in the conference, and that people become more invested in acting to the extent they have been active.

Taking the roller coaster ride together, and confirming what they really are saying out loud to each other, is what drives mutual action. When people get to this point in the conference, they *know* what they want and they *know* which others are aligned with them. Of course, they need time to set goals, divide up the work, and create a structure. If choices seem real to them at this point, they will follow through on their connections, commitments, and projects regardless of the methodology.

We have tried a number of action-planning groups – peer, mixed, voluntary, functional, and existing task forces. We have helped folks organize around a common future and related issues they identify. Every group works *if* the group

controls its own work. So we keep the tools simple too. The fancier the planning model, the harder it is for people to own it. The longer it takes to own it, the more people postpone key decisions. This is not a time for teaching new management tricks. It's a time for turning over ownership of planning to the whole conference. Simpler is better.

Two Rounds of Planning

We usually propose two rounds of planning, starting with the stakeholder groups. If folks agree with this proposal, we proceed. If not, we find out how they want to begin planning. Organizations usually like to meet in stakeholder groups or in already formed task forces to begin planning. Community or issue groups may start with stakeholder groups meeting one more time or begin immediately building voluntary coalitions around their themes.

Once we've organized into action groups, we suggest folks take ten minutes to fill out an individual planning sheet. These are personal commitments to action – to be shared only if people wish. This step also helps people collect their thoughts. In round one, groups talk over their common future and what they want to work on and with whom. They report their plans and needs for help. When everybody has heard everybody, we offer people a chance to reorganize any way they wish. We ask people to "put a stake in the ground" – to take a public stand on the issue they want to work on. Others join if they share the issue. We facilitate to make sure each person who wants to work has some others to work with. We do not decide what issues they should address.

Closing the Conference

The sponsor usually has the last word. We often close by asking those who wish to call out one or two words that reflect what they are thinking or feeling right now. Their responses would fill another book.

CHAPTER 6

Sponsoring a Future Search

How To Know When the Time is Right

> "We are caught in an inescapable network of mutuality, tied in a single garment of destiny. Whatever affects one directly, affects all indirectly."
>
> – Martin Luther King

HOW DO PEOPLE DECIDE whether to sponsor a future search? They first need to talk about the risks and benefits. How would this meeting support their organization's or their community's purposes? What about the strategic implications? Could a future search, for example, be used in the middle of a strategic planning process? Could it be run to implement a vision that already exists, or to create a shared vision? Are there shorter versions? What if old conflicts surface, and how do you get key "outsiders" to come and stay the whole time?

Facing Skepticism

We know about these concerns because we spend a lot of time on the phone discussing them. Enthusiasts often face skeptical bosses, colleagues, or clients. Some skeptics balk at the time commitment; they may be busy fighting fires and can't spare more than a day. Many fear airing dirty linen or revealing secrets. Others can't imagine a meeting without featured experts. Some wonder how a diverse group can work together, given their stereotypes of each other.

While we don't "sell" future search to anyone, we do help people decide whether they are buyers. If so, we help them muster the courage and resources to go ahead. If people have the least doubt (and even when they don't) we look with them at reasons *not* to run a future search. Is this really the right time? Have you a suitable task worth the investment? Can you raise the right crowd, and will they stay the whole time? What would you like to do with a future search that you haven't been able to do by other means?

Consider a Future Search if...	*Go Slow* when...
• A shared vision is desired	• Leadership is reluctant
• An action plan is needed	• Minimum conditions are not met
• Other efforts have stalled	• Nobody but you wants it
• New leadership is taking over	• It's a force fit to a planned meeting
• A key transition is at hand – e.g. changing markets, technology, customers, etc.	• The agenda is preconceived
• Opposing parties need to meet and have no good forum	• People have no planning time
• Time is growing short	• Everybody but you wants it – and it's your decision

Good Candidates

So far most of our conference sponsors have been interested in future search from the moment they learned about it. If people need a lot of convincing, they probably are not good candidates. About one caller in ten has the commitment, authority and resources to actually sponsor a conference. These tend to be folks who know what's needed in their organization or community. They may have participated in a future search conference, read a case study, seen a video, or talked with other sponsors. They also may be looking for new ways of working and resonate with the idea of a conference where 60 or more people can interact and plan together. Whatever caught their attention, they need no selling, only information and reassurance.

Q: WHAT AM I REALLY IN FOR IF I SPONSOR A CONFERENCE?

A: You are going to release a flood of constructive energy together with good ideas, some common directions and many willing implementers. You will also find that some old conflicts persist, though they may seem less central. You will have a lot more to work with. However, you will have to work *with* it, giving people support and assurance that you believe in what they are doing (if you do). Probably, you will find more allies for your own agendas than you thought were there. In this sense, you will have more control rather than less, because so many others are traveling the same road of their own volition. And you may end up rethinking some pet ideas that make less sense afterwards than they did before.

"I recommend this process to other communities. Even in inner cities we're talking about neighborhoods that are lagging behind, marginalized....But it takes a lot of effort. A lot of time. A lot of resources."

Wrong Time, Wrong Group

Some situations obviously are not for us. Recently we had a call from an internal consultant asking us to meet with a human resource VP who wanted to convince a CEO that their

company needs a future search, although the CEO was not asking for it. This is not a good starting place for us. We also don't know how to help folks who want future search tailored to a meeting already planned. "We've got 100 managers coming from all over the world on December 8-10. Can we do a future search?" Our answer is yes only if the decisions already made don't contradict our minimum conditions for success. Rarely is that the case. Nearly always there are other agendas – immediate problems to be solved, decisions to be ratified, proposals to be discussed, speakers to be heard.

Usually, they don't have enough time. Most likely the group is too narrow for our purposes. We know that intact groups *always* replay their customary dynamics, no matter what content, techniques or concepts are introduced. Oddly enough, our callers know this too. Indeed, the reason they *want* a future search is to change the dynamics and hopefully get more commitment.

If a meeting is already built around speakers or experts, our response is "another time." It's much harder for people to take responsibility for their own planning in a meeting where they are being told what the key issues are and what they should be doing about them. So we urge our callers to talk with folks who have sponsored conferences and to call again before they have locked in dates, agendas, and invitation list.

We are not saying people should not have other kinds of meetings, just that we have set criteria for the success of our future search model. If we agree to requests that don't fit, we know that the meeting will fall short of expectations, making interactive planning at a later time more difficult. If you want to test this method, we suggest you go all out the first time. Otherwise, ambiguous results may discourage you from trying again. That doesn't mean some of the techniques in this book can't be adapted for other purposes, like raising awareness or getting a good dialogue going. Techniques don't care what we do with them, and some of these are very good techniques. However, if you use them, think about

where you will be when the meeting is over; and don't promise more than can be done by participants in the time available.

Finding Potential Sponsors

We have no faith in speeches exhorting folks to undertake a future search. We also have found that "data" – other peoples' breakthroughs whether anecdotal or full of hard numbers – rarely move skeptics. For example, we know that a future search generates resources. Following a conference, people invest time, money, and energy in ways they had not imagined before. In following up conference after conference, we find people reporting increased budgets, foundation grants, legislative appropriations, private investment in worthy projects – all stemming from a future search. This data has *no* effect on skeptics. We retell success stories only to support people who lean toward this work and will be reassured knowing concretely what others have managed to do.

Once in a while we run an orientation session for prospective sponsors. Our experience with these is in the non-profit world – with public and private agencies that are eligible for pro bono help through our national network, SearchNet. The briefing session we like best takes about three hours and was conceived by Ralph Copleman and Skip Lange, of the Delaware Valley Area SearchNet. They get people to share their concerns, and they then describe what can and can't be done in a future search. The procedure is to invite a diverse group to brainstorm trends affecting their various communities or organizations. They don't make a mind map; they put the trends randomly on a big sheet of butcher paper. Then they ask small groups to tell what they're doing now and what they want to do in the future about the issues on the wall. The main effect is that everybody quickly learns of many things going on in the community of which they were unaware, and they see how fragmented efforts might be combined.

Planning "As If"

We often are asked to "present" future search to those who must decide whether to have a conference. Rather than just talk about something few have experienced, we offer a real time alternative: we suggest a one day planning meeting "as if" we are going forward. By the end of the day, people will know whether future search supports their goals and values and if they can turn anxiety into energy to go forward. We have had a few meetings where the planners opt out in the end, but arriving at this place together is a day well spent.

EXAMPLE

Two human resources managers from a big technology firm having key patents about to enter the public domain saw future search as a way to develop an "intellectual property" strategy. A willing corporate officer called a meeting of patent attorneys and related departments – engineering, product development, marketing, etc. We were told that this group was "ready to go." We outlined a future search and made stakeholder lists. All morning they talked about the current patent process, and what they would want out of a conference. Most became excited. By early afternoon, they were on board and had a good fix on who to invite.

The patent attorneys, however, went into a blue funk. They were not ready to rethink their interactions with the rest of the company in such a broad context. Indeed, most allowed that they were too busy, and would not have chosen to attend this meeting if it had been their decision. We recommended against a conference. They (and we) were greatly relieved that our process would not be "force-fed" to them. The meeting uncovered distress that needed attention. Our human resource colleagues became more resolved than ever to find a good opening. Eventually, they will. Were we disappointed? Well, yes. But what a narrow escape!

Which Organizations and Levels?

One flexible feature of a future search is that people with authority to plan their own meetings can run one no matter where they sit in the hierarchy. They can invite people from other levels and functions to help them. They do not need top-to-bottom sponsorship. Invited guests, no matter where they sit in a hierarchy, need not take responsibility for sponsoring the conference. In a commercial bank, for example, four departments got together on a common future because of issues raised by an information systems group. The conference was sponsored by peers and their boss was not involved. People above and parallel to the sponsors' organization were invited as guests, i.e. "outside stakeholders," who did not need to co-sponsor the event, but only show up and help the sponsor work on its future, in which they had a considerable stake. We also have seen major corporations influenced from below when upper managers attended a future search as invited guests.

EXAMPLE

In one university-based institute involving academia, government, and industry, Department A planned a future search. It stirred so much interest that the institute's director suggested it be expanded to include the whole organization. His managers, peers of the original sponsor, split on the idea, several saying they already had too much to do and wasn't this a repeat of similar events last year, etc. After some weeks of discussion, we decided to go ahead with the original conference sponsored by Department A because we really couldn't get support for anything else. The director and his team were invited stakeholders. They all showed up.

What It Takes

We think it's useful for people considering a future search to know what resources are needed. Firstly, we meet with a

"At the beginning
of the meeting I
was writing 'they'
all the time and I
found as I went
through my notes
that I started
writing 'we.'"

steering committee for a minimum of two days of meetings, and then a logistics person with administrative skills to manage invitations, site selection, meals, workbooks, and room set-up. In the simplest event, meals and breaks for as many as 64 people are required even if folks go home at night, and, for an offsite, sleeping rooms for two nights for everybody.

How costs are handled depends on the situation. Corporate sponsors and well-off non-profits usually pay all conference costs. Communities and low-budget non-profits may charge participants a nominal fee to cover expenses. Sometimes a public agency, foundation, or corporation funds the event. For our local pro bono network, we have had organizations contribute meeting space and meals in privately-owned conference centers, and have had the use of churches and schools.

Lead Time

Once a decision is made to go ahead, it usually takes three to six months to implement. Key stakeholders need enough notice so they can free up their calendars. Enough time must be allowed to find a suitable site. It's hard to sign up hotels and stakeholders around holidays, and it's easy to find stakeholders for sunny places in winter. And it may take some time to find a big meeting room with windows.

Contracting

Typically, we contract for two facilitators for six or seven days each – two or three planning days, one design day, and three conference days. This is for an optimum, no complications conference. The time can easily double for community-based meetings. Rates vary with the situation and the facilitators.

Through our social action network, we have available many folks who will work with non-profit organizations for low fees or for expenses. They are motivated by a desire for experience and a chance to join in constructive social action.

In the business world, there is no way to calculate the benefits of these meetings in economic terms. Many corporations have spent hundreds of thousands of dollars on months or years of activities that produce less long-term payoff than one three-day future search. Conferences are shelved for many reasons, but facilitator fees ought not be one of them.

We always work with a partner; there is too much going on for one person to track. We strongly prefer partnerships that reflect gender, race, and/or cultural diversity. It's good for us, and reassuring to participants. As part of our service we supply camera-ready worksheets and future-search related handouts, plus examples of participant workbooks, invitation letters, and follow-up reports from previous conferences.

Q: WHERE TO PLAN – OUR PLACE OR THEIRS?

A: Actually, our first choice is the conference site itself. Then we all know exactly what to expect, how the room will be arranged, and so on. (This practice saved us from a disastrous L-shaped room that already had been booked. We were able to move the meeting to a glass-walled atrium normally not used for meetings, but ideal for us.) Second choice is their place, so that we get some feel for the context. If we do a community conference, we want to spend time in the community. In a workplace, we like to understand the nature of the work. We have had a number of instances where the first meeting is at our place, followed by a second on site. Where to plan is not a make-or-break issue, but we recommend that you check out the conference site carefully before you are committed irrevocably.

Steering Committee

We have planned future searches with steering groups numbering as few as two people and as many as 20. The latter is more than needed, and greatly increases the time required.

In the former case, we met for two days with a CEO and VP who came to us because of a time crunch. They already had a buy-in from their staff, and they reviewed the design with others after their meeting with us. Even so, we needed two days to go through all the issues with the two of them, the same as with a much larger group.

We prefer planning with eight to ten key stakeholders (enough so we later will have at least one planner at each table). When a steering committee includes diverse stakeholders, our first meeting becomes a sort of "mini-conference." People share their goals, values, expectations, and concerns, learning from each other. We especially need diverse planners when the event is community- or issue-focused. In these conferences, the stakeholders are peers. No one group "owns" the future. So we try to have many sectors involved in the decision to go forward. If we want business leaders at the conference, for example, a Chamber of Commerce head will know how to involve them. If we need environmental or social agencies, or ethnic groups, we want to be sure we have committee members who can get the right people to come.

When an organization sponsors a conference on its *own* future, this is not such a critical issue, for "outside stakeholders" will be invited guests, not co-sponsors. We want steering committee members with decision-making authority and enough information about who the right stakeholders are. We don't need a customer in the planning meeting to get customers to the conference, but if a sponsor wants to include them, they can be a big help.

EXAMPLE

A health insurance company invited two customers and a broker to join the steering committee. The customers were surprised and delighted. They contributed thoughtful outside perspectives. Corporate staff experienced what it was like to make key decisions with people they had always kept at arms length. It was a great prelude to the conference.

Some professional planners welcome future searches. They see the meeting as a source of reliable information and a chance to share the burden and risk and to build commitment for action. Don't be surprised, though, if your expected allies turn out to be surly, tight-lipped smilers. Some planners consider these meetings a hostile incursion onto their turf. That's not so surprising when you consider how much time and effort goes into strategic planning. And we don't mean only in large corporations. Cities, towns, foundations, charities, social agencies – you find planning experts everywhere. Our goal is to join them, not beat them. It's their organization, not ours. We seek to include expert planners in meetings and to find out what they're trying to do. Their work is important to any future search conference, and the conference may give them running room they did not have before. Indeed, planners can gain a great deal of support and respect for their work in a future search. Most have no way of knowing this in advance.

Our goal is not to make strategic planners into future search junkies, just to get them to participate in their own interest. The stickiest situation is where the planners seek to upset, take over, or modify a conference desired by an executive in charge. We *do not*, repeat, we *do not* make this *our* problem. This situation existed long before we came, and will persist after we are gone. We follow The Beatles' advice: "Let it be." So we do our utmost to stick to our agenda – finding out whether this is a good time and place for a future search. In short, we want to work with committed leaders, a worthy purpose, and people with energy to act.

Chapter 6

SPONSORING
A FUTURE
SEARCH

"I want to tell you I learned more about customers in the last 24 hours than I think I ever knew."

CHAPTER 7

Planning 1

Getting Started

> "Think of organizational data as a wave, moving through space developing more and more potential explanations. If this wave meets up with one observer, it will collapse into one interpretation. All other potentialities are lost by that act of observation. An organization swimming in many interpretations can discuss, combine, and build on them. The outcome has to be a much richer sense of what needs to be done. The more participants we engage in this participative universe, the wiser we become."
>
> – Margaret Wheatley

WE USUALLY SPEND more time planning a future search than running it. The key decisions are two: selecting the task and the right stakeholders. These decisions come from a long discussion of what the sponsors hope to accomplish and how future search applies.

Steering Committee Meetings

Typically we schedule two days of meetings with a steering committee and do a lot of work by mail and phone. In the first meeting we orient folks to the conditions for success and solicit their expectations. Together, we explore the conference task, stakeholders, and time horizons. Then we re-work

our generic design and re-frame the worksheets. This "work plan" is reviewed in a second meeting and, finally, we make plans for the schedule, invitations, site, documentation, and logistics. The planning group faces an enormous amount of work to frame the task, get the right people in the room, and coordinate the event. After two days of face-to-face meetings, we usually have given them the tools to do it.

For convenience, we have organized our discussion of the planning meetings into two chapters, describing the decisions in rough sequence. In practice, we may do some of the "follow-up" agenda on the first day and/or carry on the "initial" agenda for several more meetings. We always start planning meetings with the convenors saying why they called the meeting and what they hope to accomplish. We review the agenda on the flip chart below.

PLANNING AGENDA (2 MEETINGS OR MORE)

- Future search history, theory, principles
- Stakes of people here?
 Why a conference? Why now?
- Conference Task - Is the focus an Organization?
 Community? Industry? Sector? Region?
- Design Overview
- Possible stakeholders?
 Who has information?
 Who has a stake in outcome?
 Who do we want to influence?
- Time frames: How far back & forward?
- Review Customized Design
- nvitation list (Who & how to reach them)
- Future scenario (What to include)
- Document/Communicate Outcomes
- Action Planning (Expectations)
- Logistics, Site, Workbooks, etc.

The planners tend to be unfamiliar with future search conferences. We always provide them with an overview of the conditions for success reviewed in detail in Chapter 3. We may talk about conference origins (see Chapter 4), using any or all of the same flip charts reviewed at the start of a conference (see Chapters 1 and 4). In principle we want people to know our framework, and we don't want to overload them with information.

Why A Future Search?/Why Now?

As in the conference itself, we don't do all the talking. Within the first hour we want to hear each planner talk about their stakes in the focal task. We don't feel secure until we know the committee has "crossed the bridge" from ambivalence to commitment. There is no comfort in one or two true believers and a lot of others going along for the ride. Moreover, it usually takes longer to organize a community-based conference than one sponsored by a business firm or single organization. In communities, there are many issues of sponsorship, political considerations, and uncertainty. We have known steering groups to meet weekly for months while they decide whether and how to go ahead. In hierarchical organizations with a committed person at the top, things usually go faster.

Still, there are pitfalls both in corporations and communities. Several times a CEO has sparked to future search, turned others on to the idea, and the group seemed ready to go. No matter. We still want to hear the steering group tell each other why they want to undertake this now. What benefits do they see? How much support does the CEO have?

For a community conference, we need a voluntary leadership group. The initiator might be a local non-profit organization, a government agency, a professional association, or civic group. Nearly always, they broaden the sponsorship by involving peer organizations. The conference focus might be anything from a whole community to specific issues like

education, health care, employment, housing, drugs and violence, or downtown revitalization. (We know that stakeholders raise *all* issues of concern to them in connection with *any* task.)

So we want each steering group member to talk about what their stake is in the community. What do they know about future search and how does it fit their issues? They need to hear each other to gauge the extent to which their concerns are shared. We need to hear all of them to know how much support we have for the conference.

EXAMPLE 1

A 13-year-old community technical assistance agency in New York City wanted to forge new directions with a growing list of stakeholders. In planning a conference, they uncovered an unspoken wish to celebrate their survival and growth. They decided the search was to be a coming-of-age celebration and a look at what a mature organization ought to be doing.

EXAMPLE 2

In Massachusetts, business leaders and service providers saw a manufacturing search as the last shot for survival of the sector. Facing the reality together, even in despair, they began to imagine a coalition for coordinated services – a step they never thought possible. It became a foretaste of what actually would happen in the conference.

EXAMPLE 3

A large utility's information systems director proposed future search to a deadlocked committee looking into allegations of massive waste of technology dollars. The group members were directors of divisions that use or provide information systems. The first planning day was devoted to orientation. We set a ground-rule that no decisions would be made if any person had strong reservations. In a

long "should we/shouldn't we" dialogue, the group, whose members started out protecting their own turf, became more cooperative.In a subsequent meeting with their boss, they presented unified reasons for a future search.

Reviewing the Generic Design

We always talk through our generic design (Chapter 1). We emphasize the strategic flexibility of future search. We can adapt to any point in a planning cycle, from visioning to implementation. Moreover, we do not need to rethink the whole process each time we face a new group or task. Acting on common ground and ideal futures are universal aspirations, even when people haven't the foggiest notion how to go about it.

By the time we review the background, minimum conditions, and generic design, we have done as much presenting as we want to do in one meeting and more than we do in an actual conference. From here on, the group members have to engage each other. They have to identify the conference task, stakeholders, time frames, etc. and, most important, begin taking responsibility.

What is Our Task?

After our first planning day, we may have agreement on our focus – the future of the organization, a division, or a function that cuts across divisions; the future of a community or a social issue within a community; or the future of a sector (education, health care, employment) within a region. As we refine the task, it's easier to create a list of people needed to do the job. Often, we try on a variety of tasks for size, going from local to global and back again.

In a corporation, for instance, whether the sponsor is the CEO or one department head, we have several options. We can look at the department or the whole company. We can have a conference on the future of the industry, letting

corporate stakeholders fit their own plans to the larger vision. We can search the future of the sector, e.g., systems technology, graphic imaging, planning. We can search the future of the company in its community. We can search an implementation plan for purposes already widely shared.

If we don't have agreement or if the task feels too narrow, we keeping trying alternatives.

EXAMPLE

An Information Systems group in an energy company started out to plan a conference on its own future. "Information Systems may not operate as a division in ten years", said one manager, "so why constrict our vision?" So they widened their focus to technology, with the corporation as a backdrop and information systems as an integrating function. Now everything was up for grabs. (They might have opted for the future of energy services in their region, seeking to gear information systems to the larger business.) Indeed, no matter which route they went they would explore both issues – the future of their business *and* the future of their specialty.

Community Planning and Leadership

"How do you create a language that expresses what you're here to do? Those conversations were really important. We got clarity that this was not about bricks and mortar. It was about looking at housing as a metaphor for the way we live."

In a community, we can search the future of a neighborhood, a local area, a whole town, the wider area including adjacent towns or counties; or specific issues of concern to many citizens that cut across all boundaries, like health, housing, education, and public safety. Regardless of focus, we always seek to involve a variety of citizens who don't ordinarily meet. Each time we look at a different level of task, we see a different stakeholder mix.

EXAMPLE

The Santa Cruz Community Foundation had worked for two years on affordable housing. Now they hoped to bring together all the leaders in housing to discover new possibilities. In the first planning

meeting it became clear that housing is linked to every other sector – business, employment, labor, social welfare, zoning, construction, and urban planning. The implications were that as they enlarged the context, they realized they would need stakeholders from every sector.

No matter who initiates the conference, a steering group invariably considers how to involve their neighbors. They may not start there. But as they talk about their own future, they realize it is inextricably bound up with the place across the river, the freeway, or the railroad. A common situation we encounter is adjoining cities, towns, or neighborhoods settled by different ethnic groups. The conference could be a forum for talking about their common stakes in the larger community.

As the group decides whether to have a conference, they also struggle with how to take leadership. Communities or interest groups, which are loosely-structured systems, often have no easy way to work this out. The conference task is broad and planners have diverse, sometimes competing interests. We try patiently to undo the assumption that the person who called the meeting or we as facilitators own the work. We resist the temptation to tell people what to do or to make decisions for them. And we coach people to broaden ownership lest a few folks end up doing it all and resenting the work or being resented by others later. This process of taking ownership may happen over weeks or months, not necessarily in one meeting.

"It doesn't take a lot of people to bring about significant changes. It's a matter of having a clear sense of what you want and then making movement towards that."

Describing the Task

As we decide on the central task, we look for a key phrase that captures the spirit and purpose. We keep a running brainstorm list, and may not choose a conference title for some time.

BRAINSTORMING TASKS
Example – A Computer Consulting Firm

MAIN TITLE: Forté 2005
POSSIBLE SUB-TITLES

Discovering maximum contribution

Unleashing information

Discovering true competitive advantage

Creating a shared vision

Breaking down technology walls

Creating shared vision for computing, relationships
and community

Integrating perspectives

Reaching out for common ground

Building a shared vision for a seamless partnership

Building vision for information technology leadership

TITLE CHOSEN – Forté 2005: Building a Shared Vision
For Employee, Customers, and Industry Leadership

EXAMPLES OF ACTUAL CONFERENCE TASKS

Renewing the Commitment: Corporate Accounts
Business of BC/BS of Maryland

Creating the Future: Topeka the Next 20 Years

Haworth: Quality by Design

Manufacturing and Massachusetts 2002: A Vision
of a Statewide Service System for Small and
Medium-sized Firms

The Future of Wellness in the Delaware Valley

Aligning for Action: A metro-wide conference spon-
sored by Kansas City Consensus. Working together
to become the Child Opportunity Capital

Global Risk Management 2005: Partnerships for the
Future

Coming Together as a Community around Housing:
A Search for our Future in Santa Cruz County

What are the criteria for stakeholders? We like management professor Dale Zand's concept:

- people with information;
- people with authority and resources to act;
- people affected by what happens.

Always, we ask the steering group what other criteria seem relevant to them. At some point, we may suggest options. In business conferences, we like as many levels present as possible. From supplier and customer organizations, even internal, we want influential folks who know the business. If our focus is technology or economics we may consider industry experts. If our sponsor is a non-profit agency, we push for funders and clients. If public policy looms large, we like public servants. If our focus is a community's future, we want all sectors. In addition, we always explore what demographic cross-section of local residents makes sense for the future search.

OBSERVERS

Q: A lot of people are curious about this process. Do you have room for "observers?"
A: We want folks who have an investment in the outcomes, know their relationship to the task, and will help us do the job. We discourage people who want to watch for their own reasons, or folks assigned by higher-up. This is not a make-or-break issue, just a distraction we don't need.

We know that a diverse group can put together a far richer picture of the conference focus than any one person has now. We are aware that when we don't assemble an unusual group, one that makes the planners a little anxious (and excited), it's probably not the ideal group. One pitfall is a conference in which the stakeholders have a tenuous "rela-

tionship," say, a common interest in a topic, but no practical reasons for working together. A community cultural center, for example, used a future search as a start-up meeting. It had a small staff and no real community links. Several participants showed up out of curiosity about the method or out of personal loyalty to the director. They had fun, but no investment in the center. People need some identity with the task and a desire to be involved in shaping the future.

Stakeholder Brainstorm

Our method for selecting stakeholders is relatively simple. We ask the planners to brainstorm *all* possible attendees. We emphasize that this is for discussion only, not an invitation list. We keep going until we've exhausted all groups and key people with *any* stake in the task. Here's a brainstorm list from a community housing conference:

Business	Academia
Agriculture	Health Care
Tourism	Former Residents
Builders	Homeless
Retail	Legal Community
Office Workers	Police
Small Business Owners	Youth
Environmentalists	Electeds
N1eighborhood Activists	Governmental – Bureaucrats
Cultural Groups	Newly-Married
Religious Groups	New Markets
Transportation	Commuters (both directions)
Social Services	Mental Health
Media	Union
Seniors	Banks
Farm Workers	Vacationers

Next we discuss the stakes of each group (or person) and check off those who are "essential," "desirable," and "optional." How many stakeholder groups are we talking about? The potential is infinite. We have had as few as six, as many

as 12. There are practical limits. Our ideal model is eight stakeholder groups, for then we can have eight mixed groups with one person from every stakeholder group at each table – a total of 64.

Conference size can be a frustrating matter. We've worked with as many as 100 people, and as few as 30. We like up to 64 participants for a conference large enough to influence system change and small enough for open dialogue. If the dialogue were in small groups only, we could manage hundreds of people with little constraint save physical space. In our conference we want every group to hear from every other group on every task. People have to be able to see and hear each other easily.

We have worked with nine or ten stakeholder and mixed tables under special circumstances – e.g. community conferences with many constituents. There are obvious limitations. It's harder to build community; report-outs take forever, and it is likely that important thoughts go unspoken. If you want to involve more people, consider running one conference, then enlisting participants in deciding how to involve others.

Future Search As Lightning Rod

We are resigned to the fact that future search conferences easily become lightning rods for every agenda, value, and unfulfilled dream. People with no future search experience may want to load requirements onto the event to satisfy many needs. This is okay so long as the needs don't cancel out a potential success. We are responsive and wary at the same time. Since every conference is a leap into the unknown, we need to stack our deck for success. We must not let "now or never" cloud our good judgment.

No conference is the last chance to do anything. If the task is worthy, folks will keep going and bring in more people. So we settle for "good enough" the first time, and do not set up 12 or 14 stakeholder groups, for example, until we know how to manage them. Some sponsors read this as a mixed message. "You want a broad cross-section, including a lot of

outsiders. Yet you draw the line at 64 people!" That's a fact; so far, that's the best we know how to do.

We will never know how many people are enough or what makes a "whole system." We want conference sponsors to go further than they are used to going, perhaps not to the end of the rainbow, but far enough so that important new things happen. We can combine related stakeholder groups into one table. If we need more folks, those who come this time will figure out how to bring others aboard. Future search is a learning laboratory, not a panacea. So eight stakeholder groups with eight people in each is an ideal toward which we work. Nice work if you can get it, and, as the song says, we can get it if we try. Or something close, most of the time.

Stakes Versus Demographics

"Approaching 50, it was really refreshing to have these high school students there with me looking at the same issues in the same way, out of role..."

We've thought a lot about stakeholder groups based on commitments like occupation, organization, or role and those based on natural differences like gender and ethnicity. Both possibilities exist. To isolate groups by personal traits, however, is to emphasize differences about which people have strong feelings and that cannot be altered. Our experience so far strongly parallels the research dating to World War II showing that people drop their stereotypes faster when they work on projects together.

So we recommend personal traits as criteria to ensure diversity, not to define task groups. Could we imagine conferences where folks explore an issue by age, race, gender, or country of origin? Possibly, if such categories were inescapable for our task. We would never say "never" but in general think it's a mistake to divide a future search on those lines. We rather would have a conference that reflects our community, where stakeholder groups are organized by role, function, occupation, etc., and as diverse demographically as we can make them.

Of course, issues of gender, origin, and race come up in future search conferences. These usually are raised as *community* issues, not the problem or grievance of one person or group. Our conferences have lead us to a conclusion upside-

down from the way the we used to think. Rather than a conference on "diversity" or "race relations" or "gender relations," we much prefer a conference on the community's future, as envisioned by a cross section of all citizens. Let diverse people talk to one another about what sort of community they want to live in – its health care, education, housing, safety, etc. Let them work together to imagine and act out how they want their lives to be. Under these conditions "diversity" becomes reality data, not an ideological issue.

Selecting Stakeholders

At some point we draw eight circles on a flip chart to represent stakeholder groups. Filling in the tables is the most important task our planning committee will do. The planners shape the conference by the way they identify groups, combine some, and drop others. Who to invite is a pure judgment call. We want to be mindful of a simple criterion: Will people accept their stakeholder category as reasonable?

After many weeks, the Santa Cruz County planners, who had brainstormed the long list you read earlier, settled on the following stakeholder groups:

"We tried more traditional approaches...people who were movers and shakers. We didn't have enough diversity in the room....Change really comes when the people who need it most sit with people who can help make things happen."

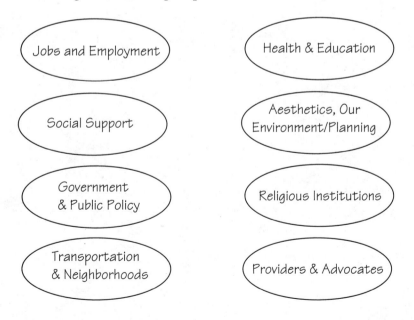

Jobs and Employment

Health & Education

Social Support

Aesthetics, Our Environment/Planning

Government & Public Policy

Religious Institutions

Transportation & Neighborhoods

Providers & Advocates

What you don't see here are the demographic criteria *also* used to insure a cross-section of the community. By design, we had teens and retirees, men and women, residents of rural Watsonville and urban Santa Cruz, wealthy executives and unemployed farm workers, AIDS and homeless activists, a local legislator, and many backgrounds including African-American, Anglo, Asian, and Latino. The steering committee made a chart with stakeholder labels across the top, and demographics down the left side. These included income, age, ethnicity, gender, and geographic location. Then they filled in every slot. They combined functional groups with shared perspectives. In the event, we had eight mixed tables and nine stakeholder groups.

PLANNING II

Finishing the Job

> "The problem of modern man isn't to escape
> from one ideology to another...our problem
> is to live in the presence and in the attributes
> of reality. Then we will be able to put the
> picture together. This picture can only be the
> outcome of all the empathy given to many
> things observed in common. When many
> things are observed in common by the many
> who constitute a society, we will have
> reached a condition worth celebrating."
>
> – Frederick Sommer

WE NEED from one to several follow-up planning meetings to complete a future search agenda. Here are the major agenda items that remain once the task and stakeholders have been selected:

- Time frames: how far back and forward
- Review customized design
- Invitation list: who and how to reach them
- Future scenario: what to include
- Document/communicate outcomes
- Action planning: expectations
- Logistics: site, workbooks, etc.

The next major steering committee decision is how far back and how far forward will we search? The answers determine how we structure our review of the past. It may also affect the conference title if the future date is to be included.

Reviewing the Past: How far back?

To organize a review of the past, we create three time lines divided into three or four "eras." Eras can be related to (1) the age of "X," (2) critical events in the life of "X," and (3) the age of the oldest conference participants. "Default" eras are the mid-60's, -70's, -80's, and now. If we have no good rationale for other time frames, we use the defaults.

EXAMPLE

A four-year-old company in a young industry assured us that it made little sense to review the '60's. The president was born in 1963, the planning group's mean age was 32, and there would be few stakeholders over 40. The planners couldn't see going back before 1975. We encouraged them to leave the door open so that the few over-40's could add what they knew about the start of the industry. We calibrated our time line as pre-1970, 1970-79, 1980-89, 1989, and now because the company was formed in 1989. Here all time frames applied globally and personally. For the conference focus we reviewed the industry's history, and asked people to add data about the company's four-year life.

The Ideal Future: How far forward?

A related decision is how far forward to project "X's" future. To free ourselves from current reality we have to access our dreams, wishes, and ideals *as if they are feasible*. The larger the change and the faster we want to make it, the less feasible it becomes. Fighting fires, managing crises, we rarely stop to ask whether what we're doing now begets more of the

same or moves us toward an ideal future. Going further into the future, say 10 to 20 years or more, has important consequences for feasible short term action steps.

We learned this from the late Ed Lindaman, NASA planning director for the first moon shot. On the way to the moon, Ed liked to say, the astronauts made tiny course corrections. Because the moon is 250,000 miles away, it only took small course corrections early in the flight to hit the moon. There are two benefits in projecting a future search as far ahead as the planners can tolerate. First, released from present constraints, we dream larger dreams. Second, we can make smaller (therefore more doable) course corrections next week. So we urge our steering committee as far into the future as they are willing to go. Ten years out is a reasonable target. Twenty is even better. Shorter time frames tug us toward problem-solving, keeping us from saying where we really want to go. Small changes now will get us to the moon if we can decide together where the moon is!

EXAMPLE

A newly-public corporation chose a five-year time horizon. As the conference reached common ground on a host of issues, a disagreement created high anxiety. Many in the room thought it was unrealistic to go as far as their 5-year scenarios called for. Talking it over at the end, they said 10 years seemed attainable. So we changed our time frame retroactively, increasing the probability that doable steps now would have a big impact later.

Conference Dates

We need three months or more from the first meeting to organize a future search conference. That's if everything goes like clockwork. People fill their calendars months in advance. Desirable places are hard to reserve. Groups that want a conference now may settle for a less-than-optimum stakeholder mix and/or a sub-optimal meeting place. We urge

sponsors to pay attention to the time they need to get the people they really want, since every person will open up new actions.

There is a related calendar consideration – finding a meeting place. We prefer off-site locations with a chance for recreation. When people stay together they build community more quickly. The closer we schedule to holidays and vacation times the longer in advance we have to book. We may need up to six months to get a meeting room with windows (the only kind we can work in).

OFFSITE MEETINGS

Q: Must you always meet off-site? Can people go home at night?
A: Escaping distractions is a luxury that pays off. However, this is *not* a make-or-break issue. We have run good conferences where people go home at night, meeting in schools, colleges, churches, or other local facilities. We can do our work so long as people commit to the whole conference.

Finalizing the Stakeholder List

Now it's time to finalize the stakeholder invitation list. The steering committee must select specific people who meet their criteria. Alternates may need to be identified in case first choices can't make it. Sometimes, stakeholder groups can be asked to send volunteers.

EXAMPLE

To recruit for an industrial plant conference, the manager told team members and leaders that anyone who wanted to come was invited. They had room for one team leader and three team member tables. They filled the tables with volunteers, guaranteeing commitment and enthusiasm. (When we have more volunteers than slots, we suggest a lottery.)

Q: Do stakeholders represent their organizations?
A: We never consider future search participants as "representing" anybody, except themselves. They bring important information, viewpoints, and experience as stakeholders. We think it's unrealistic to assume they can commit people who aren't there.

Invitations

Once we know the date, place, and specific stakeholders, the committee sends out invitations quickly. Invitations can be long or short, a one-time mailing or several mailings, and may involve personal phone calls. A lot of thinking goes into getting people the steering group really wants.

Sometimes sponsors assume their stakeholders won't show up, stay, or spend time talking about, say, the past. They imagine certain people are too busy, important, or knowledgeable to need this meeting. Even if they came, they would never agree on what to do, etc. We always test these assumptions. Folks new to future search may compromise key components before they have any experience. The alternative to compromise is to arm the inviters with as much information as they need to advocate effectively.

"I felt honored when Herm called and asked me to come. I asked him who I should be representing, and he just said, 'How about being Joe?' I said, 'Great, I can do that!.'"

So far all the conferences we've worked with have raised the "right" crowd. In a business school, conference planners sent out one puzzle piece a week for five weeks. To get the sixth and last piece, people had to show up. What was the last piece of the puzzle? *"You! "* In a community manufacturing conference, policy makers and company presidents were considered essential. They asked a U.S. Senator to lend his support in a luncheon speech. He agreed to tell how he would follow-up on the output. Publicizing his commitment helped get key people to attend. Naturally, we'd rather have had him participate in the conference. However, a luncheon speech insured the right people were in the room and a valuable ally for follow-up had been confirmed. What we don't want are

long keynote or closing speeches, nor even short ones by people who don't participate in the conference.

Sometimes steering committee members visit key people and invite them face-to-face. Often they divide up this work, following up people they know personally. One useful technique is for the steering committee to brainstorm a list of the benefits to stakeholders of their attending the conference. Here's an actual example:

Benefits to Stakeholders

- Ability to influence.
- Opportunity to meet neighbors, leaders, and folks with shared interests.
- Can contribute and learn at the same time.
- Participation in a leading edge process.
- Opportunity (business firm) to meet other employees, vendors, customers to gain additional perspectives to improve their own performance.
- Learn more about challenges facing us and help define ways to meet them.
- Opportunity to help influence strategy.
- Create ways to leverage information use and delivery as a competitive advantage.
- Identify areas of commonalty and diversity.
- Influence the direction of the whole community.

"We invited people that we thought were creative, concerned, and interested in their community; people who might be willing to give some time to something like this."

We advise steering committees to tell those invited what benefits they can expect if they attend, and to ask if there are barriers to their participation that the steering committee can help remove. We like to let people know that this will be a safe, enjoyable, and valuable experience. The box opposite shows how one group anticipated these issues before making phone calls.

PLANNERS IN ACTION

The Santa Cruz community planning group worked out answers to these questions before making phone calls to solicit attendance:

1. Why was I invited to participate?
2. What does housing have to do with me?
3. Why must I be there the entire 2 ½ days?
4. What will I have to do if I come?
5. Who else will be participating?
6. What will be the outcome to this conference?
7. I can't come. Can I send someone to take my place?
8. Is so-and-so invited? Why not?

When a Good Idea Becomes a "Have-To"

After finishing this chapter, we began rethinking the origins of some of our planning practices. We worried that this book, rich in details from our own experience, would become a literal blueprint. Procedures, especially creative ones, can be exceedingly seductive. If you watch the way a standard design evolves, you quickly see how a creative idea can turn into rote repitition. The pattern goes like this: a planner for a conference on quality says, "Why not have people bring something that symbolizes quality? This would help them become invested in the conference." Says another, "Great idea!" To which we add, "Okay, but how and when would you use what people bring?" A long discussion follows. Finally, it is agreed that when people introduce themselves at the start they can show their quality symbol and tell why they brought it. We do that, and the ensuing activity, which takes no more than 15 minutes, creates a wonderful sense of shared purpose, exactly what the steering committee intended.

Now, here's where the fun begins. The next time we plan a conference, we say, "What do you think about having people bring an artifact or symbol to the conference? We could use it as part of the getting acquainted session at the start." The steering committee now wants more information. Why? What? Is it essential? What should we bring? An hour long discussion ensues, on a wrinkle that is not essential to the success of our conference and that, in this instance, is supplied by us, not by the steering committee. Suddenly, we have taken a situation-specific good idea from one conference and made it a feature of our generic design. We have also added significantly to the length of our planning meeting.

We have another example. In a corporate conference some years ago, the steering committee, uneasy with the idea of letting people imagine an ideal future in whatever way they wish, decided they'd like to "prompt" people with a list of the kinds of features they'd like to hear addressed: size, structure, dollar volumes, and product lines in addition to relationships, policies, and so on. (In the event, no future scenario groups address all these issues, nor do they need to for the future search to succeed.) In any case, putting these prompts into the worksheet reduced the steering committee's anxiety. In no time at all, we had built into our planning a new steering committee task: working out their own prompts for the future. Now, this is not a bad thing, for it does help the steering group set more concrete expectations. Is it a make-or- break design feature? We doubt it. On balance, we think it helps future scenario groups focus their work.

We can point to many examples of specific adaptations for particular circumstances that we have not put in our generic design. However, the temptation exists, and we have to resist standardzing every variation lest we end up one day with a set of tasks that no longer carry out our original purposes – to put responsibility more firmly in the hands of our participants.

News Clips and Memento/Artifact Museum

We also ask that people bring a current magazine article or news story on a trend they believe is affecting the future of the conference topic. They will be asked to discuss what they brought when we start looking at the present.

Many steering groups (see above) ask participants to bring an artifact, story, or item that is personal and symbolic of their relationship to the conference topic. Tangible items start people thinking about the meeting before they arrive. People discuss these articles at the start of the conference. The items have been funny, intriguing, interesting, touching, and always effective in forming a community quickly. If this step is taken, it needs to be a steering committee decision, based on what they consider appropriate to the task.

Reviewing the Detailed Design

Between planning meetings we adapt our conference design to the steering committee's decisions. In a later meeting we go over this work plan in detail. We reiterate the tasks, goals, roles, etc. This review gives us a chance to talk over last-minute concerns and confirm our working agreement with the committee.

Future Scenario Prompts: What Should We Include?

A major future search task calls for participants to imagine their ideal future and prepare a creative presentation. The planning committee may suggest some features they would like to see addressed in these scenarios. It is desirable to have people visualize their ideal community, corporation, or network as concretely as they can, imagining that they already have created what they want. (See box for actual examples.)

PROMPTS FROM VARIOUS CONFERENCES

COMMUNITY CONFERENCE

1. Put yourself into the future. Look back to 1994. Visualize and describe the community you *really* want as if you are living in it *now*, in 2005.

2. List your *accomplishments* since 1994, with special reference to:
 - Nature of community leadership
 - Mix of population
 - Types and location of housing
 - Zoning and planning policy
 - Financing methods for new and existing projects
 - Employment opportunities
 - Relations between county and university
 - Community services and facilities
 - Transportation
 - Relations between north and south county areas
 - Public policies, community initiatives
 - Other highly-desirable features

CORPORATE CONFERENCE

In your dramatization cover:
- Achievements of the last 5 years
- Structure, size, $ volumes, and product lines
- Notable policies, procedures, systems, and values
- Outstanding features of the company as a place to work
- Customer relations
- Relations with the community
- Other highlights you consider extremely desirable

Documenting the Conference

There are good reasons to document a conference. One is to provide participants with a record of what they did and a reminder of commitments made. Another is to help people who didn't attend understand what happened. A surprising amount of work gets done in less than three days, and the results are often dramatic. For example, we've seen strangers from labor, government, and business build a coalition. We've seen boards of directors redefine their roles – something they could never do before. We witnessed the birth of an implementation plan for a city vision involving every neighborhood. We watched in wonder as mistrustful parties to a corporate merger produced a shared vision and mission. When people find alignments they never thought existed, their stories are worth telling. Our communities and corporations could stand a little good news about meetings.

At the same time, the full power of a future search can't be experienced second hand. People who did not attend can't be expected to make the same internal shifts and commitments as those who have worked through the past and present together. We can, however, show them issues that were worked on, the common ground achieved, and the action commitments made. And we can, if we plan it, involve others in covering the same ground in a later conference or in shorter meetings.

Here are some ways to think about documentation. Is the goal of our document to inform only, or is it also to involve others in future actions? Most conferences prepare a written document from data gathered in real time. It can range from typing up flip charts and action plans to a narrative report. We prefer the latter. Flip charts don't mean much except to the people who created them, unless they are presented with a written narrative.

We've seen everything from newspaper formats to four-color reports, with photos, charts, graphs and artwork. The objective is *not* to give somebody else an experience they can only have for themselves. It's to tell them what was done,

what was learned, what plans are underway, and how – if that is a goal – they can join the parade.

Media Coverage

Should news, radio, or TV reporters be invited to cover a future search? If they come as stakeholders, participate in it, and write a story afterwards, we say "yes." If they want to show up in the middle, interview people on what happened the first day, and put it the morning paper, we say "no." What little coverage we have seen before and during the event usually misses the point entirely. Journalists rarely have future search experience. They tend to be cynical about large public meetings, involving a cross-section of interests with an apparently-vague agenda. Their cynicism is well-founded; they cover a lot of talky meetings with high-sounding agendas, often involving some of the same people. They have no reason to believe this one is different.

If coverage is planned, we need to be thoughtful about what constitutes real news. One possibility is to invite reporters to the last session, the action planning, at the point where people make public their goals and plans. Another is to invite the press to interview people after the conference. Our wish is that these conferences be covered in terms of what they mean to the people who participated in them, once those people have had a chance to act. Until then, the story is only good intentions, confusion, and nothing much else. The best stories are written weeks or months later, when the conference impact has become a reality. Our fear is that some insensitive journalists, short of any actual outcomes, will cover the techniques and process, dismiss them as "soft," and discount the hard impact because it's not visible yet.

Integrating Technology

Increasingly, people want to wed new technologies to future search. Many folks are interested in how to use computers, for example, both to display data during the conference and to record flip charts. We are very cautious about

this. We don't want to do anything that takes participants away from conversing with each other. This is *much* more important than having a comprehensive record of what was said.

The point is that we are creating an environment for dialogue, and this environment includes walls papered with flip charts created by the participants which remain for the duration. These charts shape the dialogue and reflect their interpretations and agreements. Overheads or computer screens that come and go *cannot* substitute for this function. Indeed, to use machines to flash charts briefly (as in a corporate data dump) is to lose the main point of our work. This will be true even if each person is immediately handed a print out. This event isn't over until its over. While we're in progress, we like all the output in plain sight, not in a computer file, not in a drawer, and not sitting in little piles around the room.

EXAMPLE

At one conference we agreed to experiment with a new technology, useful for documenting meetings. A non-participating recorder with a lap-top computer sat at every table noting flip chart contents. The benefit was a compiled list of report-outs in everyone's hands at the end of the conference. However, having one-eighth of our participants working as typists struck us as too high a price to pay. We liked the output but believe that one or two typists at a small table could do it as well. (In Harrison Owen's Open Space meetings, for example, people bring laptops if they wish. A room is set aside for typing up notes *after* each session. Volunteer participants do the job, and the output is distributed at the end of the conference, or daily if facilities allow. Flip charts remain on the walls.)

We believe what happens within and between people will influence participant behavior no matter what form the docu-

mentation takes. If these important shifts do not happen, no amount of documentation will make them happen after the fact. We also are aware of the extent to which technologies – e.g. overhead projectors, films, computers – can be used to insulate us from chaos, anxiety, and confusion. So we guard against attractive substitutes for true engagement. We do not want to compromise any of the critical dynamics of a future search.

Video

Many sponsors arrange to videotape their conference. A 10-15 minute video can capture the energy and emotion of the experience even better than written words. A 20-30 minute video can go more deeply into the content, tracking particular stakeholders through the three days. However, 16 hours of unedited tape is useless. You need a crew that knows the production process and how work with large interactive groups. They must know how to recede into the background and not intrude on the work. With a skilled crew, participants forget about the cameras in the first few minutes.

Gifts

Gifts for participants are, of course, optional. For reasons we cannot fathom, everyone loves T-shirts. We still wear our "I am a CRE stakeholder" shirts to go with our Forté Systems baseball caps.

Logistics and Participant Workbooks

Conference administrators always perform a critical job and can use all the help they can get. Here are some administrative tasks:

- Finding sites
- Food
- Lodging
- Transportation

- Meeting room set-up, flip charts, etc.
- Participant registration
- Participant workbooks
- Reproducing worksheets and handouts
- Participant list
- Creating mixed tables
- Supplies for future scenarios

A sample workbook appears in Appendix B. Details on materials and room set-up appear in Appendix A. At this point we are ready to go. For conferences close to home, we'll arrive on opening day. If we have to travel far, we come in a day earlier. And we always check before leaving home to make sure our supplies have arrived.

If we have done a good job of planning, we have sowed the seeds for success. Now we can now turn all of our attention to facilitating the meeting.

CHAPTER 9

Facilitating

How to Manage the Roller Coaster

> "If you always do what you always did, you
> always get what you always got."
>
> – Anon

THE PURPOSE OF OUR FACILITATION is to help people resolve the struggle between old patterns and new paths. We do this by:

- Keeping the conference task front and center;
- Encouraging self-management and responsibility;
- Staying with uncertainty in ourselves and in the group until people decide what they will and will not do together.

Focusing on Purpose

The purpose of a future search is to evolve a common future for an organization or community and develop self-managed plans to move toward it. When participants have other agendas, we hear them but don't work with them. We are *not* "process consultants" on interpersonal dynamics. We

don't lead exercises where people stand back and examine their own behavior. We don't ask people why they do this or that. We don't take positions except on the overall goal, which becomes the anchor point for our work. We don't teach or preach. When participants do any or all of the above during a future search, we listen. We don't react. We are facilitators in the narrowest sense. Our job is to keep people moving toward action on a common future.

A major basis for our work is the Emery/Trist discovery that putting tasks into a global context and supporting self-management reduces the tendency to fight or flee. This insight is the most effective way we know of reconciling the differing demands of a complex task, the dynamics of diverse groups, and the values of a democratic society.

"It was different from any conference I've ever gone to. I think the facilitators were very skilled in allowing it to be the people's conference and not their conference."

Still, anything can happen. Groups manage task anxiety in lots of ways. Flight/fight and dependency are just the tip of the iceberg. Facilitating purposeful work means making it acceptable for people to keep working on the task even when they feel anxious. (This is in contrast to dialogue and community-building groups where the anxiety and underlying assumptions may be explored at length.) Should a whole conference decide that continued work is pointless, that they have no common ground, for example, we would stop. That hasn't happened yet. But it could. Our general rule is to deal with what is happening, not what our theory says *should* happen, and to treat what actually goes on as the only reality that matters.

We make space for what folks want to say. We don't make assumptions about what they could or should say. We accept each person's right to sit on or to reveal whatever *they* consider relevant. That puts people in charge of their own experiences and reactions.

Encouraging Self-Management

A group of six to eight can organize its own work without a facilitator at their table when the task and deadlines are clear. One simple aid is the "self-manager guide." We sug-

SELF MANAGER GUIDE

- DISCUSSION LEADER
- TIME KEEPER
- RECORDER
- REPORTER

gest (but do not insist) that each group divide up the work, using a discussion leader, time keeper, recorder, and reporter. If they do, half the group immediately shares leadership. If they rotate just once, every person in the room will have a leader role before the second day is over.

This largely unobserved sharing of the load should not be minimized. Shared self-management contributes significantly to the success of the hard work people do, the visible amount of output they produce, and the high degree of implementation that follows future searches.

Our role is to enable those results *and* to stay out of the way. If a small group is struggling, we become involved only if they invite us. So long as people carry out their tasks, it is not necessary for them to have elegant process skills. Our job is to attend to whatever is in front of our noses. We feel most secure when unexpected incidents can be viewed as "current reality," accepted as such, and not be identified as something the facilitators must fix. We are most at risk if we attempt to solve "problems" without consulting the group.

EXAMPLE

In one future search the walls filled with data about
the past. It was a large group, we were using vertical
charts, and there was no limit on how much people
could put up. The first morning we ran out of wall
space. As people worked on the second task, we –
the facilitators – began moving flip charts around.
Our rationale was (a) we're saving time, and (b)
we're doing a needed, but trivial, task. (We could
also add, now, (c) we're relieving our own anxiety
over this unexpected development.) After a coffee
break, the room had "changed." Stuff wasn't where
it had been the last time people looked up. Sud-
denly, the data belonged more to us than to the
participants. "Where is such-and-such?" asked
somebody. "Well," we said," it's over there." We
were justifying our decision. Now, if we see a prob-
lem that could affect everybody, we make a public
announcement to that effect, and ask the group if
they want to solve it.

Staying With Uncertainty

Our biggest challenge is not visible to participants. We
think of it as staying with the uncertainty people feel when
facing a whole that is much more complex than the pieces
each person was aware of. Margaret Wheatley (1992), who
has run many future searches, has shown how open systems
that engage their environment continue to grow and evolve.
Part of this process is making order out of complexity,
something we can't do unless we experience the complexity.

Moreover, *our* anxiety intensifies when we hold off con-
clusions or solutions. Nobody likes uncertainty; the natural
tendency is to reduce it as fast as possible. Indeed, the
function of most consulting techniques is exactly that, but in
a future search, we take a different tack. We allow ourselves
to stay confused in the midst of apparently chaotic informa-
tion. In fact, each task opens up more unspoken concerns,

beliefs, and fantasies. These exist in every group as a reality quite separate from what is true or false.

Ambiguity rises fast when a group lets out so much of what is usually kept hidden. So we encourage people to give concrete examples of what they mean. That helps all of us ground ourselves in each others' realities. Because it's our job to live with uncertainty and not "fix" it, we hold off solutions until action planning time

To the extent that we don't take negative *or* positive comments personally, others are less likely to do so. We know such comments derive from what is going on in the conference context; they have nothing to do with our goodness or badness as people. We hear a spectrum of reactions to every comment; and people modify and defend every imaginable position. We have seen some folks flip between extremes in an eyeblink.

These twists and turns make everyone nervous, including us. For participants to be free to travel such tricky terrain with strangers or adversaries requires a safe enough container. "Safe enough" means we don't judge (out loud) what anybody says. Whether we agree or disagree is irrelevant. We may put in our two cents late in a conference when most of the issues are on the table. When we do, it always takes the form of how we view what is being discussed. (Example: "What I see is agreement between you on point A and opposing views on B. Is that it?")

Managing Informal Subgroups

In facilitating future searches, we have found Yvonne Agazarian's theory of systems-centered group dynamics extremely valuable. Her theory describes how the same dynamics of change occur whether we look at ourselves, at society, or any system in between. We all survive, develop, and transform by owning and integrating differences rather than by stereotyping, attacking, or isolating them (Agazarian & Janoff, 1993).

One level of group transformation is easy to describe:

"One thing that really opened my eyes..there's a lot of similarities from the team leaders to the staff, to the 'outsiders,' to the team members."

people realize they can live with their positive and negative feelings at the same time. In a future search we open the door to that realization, giving those who wish a chance to go through it. The more we as facilitators learn to live with our own contradictions and polarities, the easier it is for us to open that door by validating whatever people bring up. So it takes some self-knowledge to facilitate this event. The more we experience our own potential for faulty assumptions, stereotyping, low trust, and avoidance of anxiety, the easier it is for us to accept that this is where new groups usually start. The more we can live on the edge of uncertainty and just wait, the better prepared we are to stay with a group's struggle. We have found that somebody in every conference knows what needs to be said. We keep the door open for them when we listen without acting. That way we help a group shift toward active dialogue, reality checking, and creative collaboration.

That is why we consider the ability to accept the roller-coaster ride as central to the success of a future search. It is one of the few times people ever get a chance consciously to hold the tension between life's ups and downs. The journey into action takes a group to the depths of despair and the heights of elation. But we finish the conference in neither place. Rather, most people come to a balanced reality, talking at last about common ground, unresolved issues, and what we are now willing to do together.

Agazarian shows how simply we can disrupt expected patterns and keep the ups and downs in fruitful tension. One key technique is to uncover emotional subgroups for people who dissent from what is being said, that is, to find out who is in the same boat. Subgroups, in this sense, are latent. Neither we nor the participants know how many there are. Emotional subgroups exist independently of stakeholders and mixed groups. Indeed, people form subgroups across all boundaries without knowing it. So we can be sure that dissenters rarely sit alone with their thoughts and feelings.

People tend to form subgroups around stereotypes and untested assumptions. They look for others they perceive are

like them. They may enjoy statements that support their stereotypes and ignore those that don't. It is common in meetings for one vocal person to keep the illusion that he or she speaks for everybody while a bunch of others seethe and feel impotent. It is equally common for somebody to speak up believing they stand alone and nobody cares.

We seek allies for every point of view so that each person's reality is validated. In his consensus experiments, Solomon Asch (see Chapter 4) found that just one ally would enable people to stay true to their own reality. Without an ally, people can coerce themselves into agreeing with propositions they know to be false or values they don't hold. This becomes important when somebody in a large group dialogue contradicts what most other people are saying. Nearly always anxiety rises. We sense the electricity in the room. Will we now have conflict? Our first impulse might be to smooth over the tension, dismiss it, or try to dissuade the non-conformist.

Supporting Contrarians

Instead, we have learned to welcome contrary remarks as advancing the future search task. They give people an opportunity to modify their stereotypes and assumptions for themselves. All we need do is accept every statement as part of the shared reality. Like it or not, this comment is how some one of us feels, sees, hears, believes, or thinks. And that is a reality we cannot deny if we want to work together. We – the folks in this room – are all we've got, warts and all. We have no choice but to consider every statement part of the common pool. More, these statements give folks a chance, if they wish, to explore the other side. This principle makes our job much easier. We don't need to diagnose a group, or an individual, or to fix any situation. We need only to hear the shifting discussion. We need not act on every comment. This dynamic is especially important when the conference confronts its common future, just before action planning.

"This was a safe environment where people can reveal their experiences and not have to defend ourselves or attack. I got a tremendous amount of insight when we got to share what's significant to us and we didn't have to defend ourselves about it."

Validating Polarities

In addition, groups tend to connect to the "all good" or "all bad" aspects of life and temporarily forget that there's another side. That way a group gets rid of the part people unconsciously don't want to own just then. It is common in future search conferences for folks to put up one negative trend after another for 20 minutes or more. Eventually, somebody notices and says, "How come there's nothing positive on our list?"

People who bring up opposites make key contributions to the conference. They are often in touch with another aspect of reality. Listening to them, without having to do anything, is one way participants learn that they can carry on despite their differences. So we make sure that a group does not scapegoat contrarians. Our rule-of-thumb is that no one goes out on a limb without our inquiring who else has the same view.

We also check our tendency to jump on a bandwagon that would deny or soften any polarity. You will not hear *us* say things like, "Well, so far we have all negative trends. Let's put up some positive ones." A group member may say that, but not us. Instead, we are more likely to ask, "Does anybody have anything to add?" We always let information, and the "positive" and "negative" values put on it, emerge from the group.

We value that controversial positions become public. We don't "work" them. Trying to negotiate a resolution, worthwhile work in other settings, is a waste of energy in a future search. As differences become part of our reality and enough people feel less suspicious, shy, stubborn, or threatened, they begin to experience that there isn't "one right way" to a desired future. They find surprising overlap in what they want, regardless of why they want it or how they want to proceed. They also experience how much collective energy they have if they accept each other as they are. To the extent people can live with polarities, they can act on common ground.

SOME OTHER THINGS WE DON'T SAY

"Well, at this point you should all be feeling pretty
 helpless and scared."

"We've been to the depths. Now it's time to go to the
 heights."

"We've heard a lot about the environment. How come
 nobody has mentioned family life?"

"The next task is great. You're gonna love it!"

"Compared to other groups, you are much more (or
 less)_____."

"We asked you to note two or three items. How come
 you did six?"

"Do you really think it's as bad as all that?"

Write your own example:

Conflict

There are dilemmas and risks in putting conflict on hold. Some folks may use their deeply-felt differences as a rationale for not doing anything. So pervasive is the culture of conflict management, so widely-known the therapeutic value of "putting it all on the table," that many people have come to believe they can't do *anything* without getting into all their conflicts. While the impulse is admirable, indulging it is fatal to a future search. For one thing, it's based on a false assumption. If we couldn't do anything until we delved into our deepest disagreements, people would hardly get through a day with their families, co-workers, fellow drivers on the highway, or shoppers at the supermarket. We do not need to "work" every issue in daily life.

Granted, a future search provides a rare opportunity to engage others face-to-face. However, it also provides a rarer and more precious opportunity – to do something constructive *right now*. We do not mean to avoid, bury, or deny conflict. We mean only to contain it, to invite people to put on

the back-burner what they have not been able to resolve until now in favor of what is *already* resolved; that which they could not act on before because they never had access to each other. Such are the paradoxes of a future search conference. As facilitators it falls to us to both support and confront the urge to fight when it threatens the conference's purpose.

Supporting Second Thoughts

We see the urge to replay disagreements most clearly at the moment when people must confirm their common future just prior to action planning. Nearly always one or a few members of a group will raise issues that separate and divide. Sometimes they nit-pick the language, sometimes they surface substantial value conflicts. "What do we mean by 'families'?" someone will say, for example. "Do we include all loving relationships or only traditional nuclear families?"

In a sense, this is another form of a "should we/shouldn't we" dialogue, like the one that preceded the decision whether to have a conference in the first place. People are at a decision point: whether to keep fretting over what is unresolved or to commit to what is possible now. Tension rises as a group seeks to rework, or alternatively to duck, the tough stuff brought up. Our position at these moments is unequivocal. We believe the dialogue is *essential* to the success of our conference.

Before they can commit, people need to express reservations, skepticism, or reluctance to go along with what others want. It is equally essential that we not reopen the issues as if we are now going to resolve them. Any sticky issue that comes up near the end of a conference is one that we are unlikely to resolve at this juncture.

Facilitating in Tense Moments

Our facilitation of the common future dialogue has three aims. One, we want to allow enough time – usually an hour – for the whole group to say whatever is on their mind about their common future. A second is to make sure that if a

disagreement surfaces we have heard the various sides. We don't want lone dissenters hanging out on a limb. They are rarely alone in their thoughts, and everyone is helped by reality data – who else has this issue. A third aim is to reaffirm that we are here to help people work on issues they feel ready, willing, and able to tackle *now*.

A group may persist in going deeper into its differences. As facilitators we can't make people do what they don't want to do. If the conference doesn't come to a spontaneous resolution in 15 minutes or so, we point out the dilemma. We can also make clear that the choice is theirs, and we will respect it. Each conference resolves this dilemma in its own way. One obvious resolution is for the parties to set aside time in the future to really tackle the issue.

EXAMPLE

In conference on reducing infant mortality, the group surfaced strong feelings about competition for funds, beneath which were deeper concerns on sensitive matters like race, gender, power, and control. In a follow-up meeting, two months later, drawing on norms of open communication and respect for others' opinions, participants went more into what they needed to do to sustain the momentum for family-centered, neighborhood-based infant care.

This is far from conflict management. We are not seeking a resolution of differences. Rather, we want to be unlocked from stereotyped assumptions about who is willing to do what, capable of knowing what we can and can't control, holding in check the impulse to force our views on others, and exploring choices we didn't have before.

Barriers

There are other barriers future search groups face. One is making assumptions about people who seem different. We may stereotype others as players of power games or hostile

adversaries, as misinformed or all-powerful, wise, or be-nevolent. Acting on stereotypes, we protect or align our-selves with our imagined friends/foes through compliance, aggression, or stonewalling. One unique aspect of future search is the way our pattern of work helps those who are ready to take down the barriers for themselves. By "pattern" we mean the pooling of information – the small group discussions, public reports and dialogues – which enable everyone to say what needs to be said.

We see people dismantling barriers in each task. They do this in various ways – by finding acceptable traits in those seen as different, by sharing leadership and reducing status differences, by listening and being heard. None of this happens suddenly or across the board. Rather we slowly accumulate new perceptions that complicate the old ones. Every time a group moves through a barrier, there's an unleashing of blocked energy. In a matter of hours those who move from complaining and blaming to owning up and finding new allies also discover that significant action becomes possible.

Authority Dynamics

We set up a new temporary community for each future search. It's a relatively flat structure, but not without authority figures. The sponsors represent one kind of authority. And we represent another, since we are up front from the start. Moreover, we know future search dynamics better than most; after all, it's our game board. Still, the decisive moves belong to the other players. How we use our authority affects this system. We believe that action breakthroughs come with "real-time" shifts in relations among stakeholder groups. These shifts becomes more likely if we relate to the group as a "dependable authority." That means we provide information folks don't have, start and end sessions on time, reiterate overall goals, manage large group dialogues, and back out when the group is working.

We do not pretend we have no authority. We are mindful of the power that goes with center stage. We know well the

temptation to serve by doing for people what they can do for themselves. Or to treat every suggestion as a problem we should solve. Above all, we have to watch our tendency to take group frustration personally and withdraw or clamp down. We work hard to sit on our own wishes to control the uncertainty, minimize conflict, squash differences, and keep everybody happy. We contain our own fantasies that *this* group will fly apart if we don't keep the lid on. We struggle to put aside our needs to be loved, appreciated, and all-wise. We have to trust that out of apparent chaos these folks who may be confused, bewildered, excited on Day 1 and Day 2 will create order on Day 3, so long as conditions for discovery are maintained.

So we seek to minimize authority dynamics by shifting attention from us onto the task. Participants work as peers on simple, self-managed tasks. They interact with each other far more than with us. They share leadership roles. The tasks are empty bottles into which people pour perceptions and experiences. Still, it would be foolish for us to believe that groups don't act out authority issues with us. There is always an undercurrent of dependency. Many people unconsciously deny their ability to learn and to make decisions, especially in the early stages of a conference. (Just as some facilitators deny their privileges and responsibilities.) Groups may look to us for enlightenment: "Now, here are the three most important things we have learned from looking at the past." Some folks become visibly annoyed when we don't provide as much clarity as they want. So they may flee into complaining, problem-solving, or getting coffee.

If we minimize power struggles between us, and between us and the group, there will be fewer tugs-of-war at the tables. Defiant groups attack each other if they can't take shots at the leader. We are there to be shot at and will be. It's no fun, but it's no big deal either. If we don't fall dead and we don't shoot back, we will have a quick truce, followed by a peace treaty. So we accept everything we hear as something this community needs to deal with.

Boundaries

A key part of our work is maintaining boundaries of time and task. These boundaries make it easier for folks to contain frustration and turn it into creative energy. Without boundaries we could not accomplish complex tasks with large groups. If we muddy our boundaries, we muddy our purpose. We are mindful that it's easy to let time slip and then justify it as a "need." We don't pretend that we can extend one task without short-changing another. We have only 16 hours or so to meet our goals.

We therefore invite people to share responsibility in a way that few groups ever do. They have to discipline themselves to work the tasks in the time available, and to manage themselves so that each person who wants to speak has a chance. That means some people can't say everything they want to say. At the same time, we increase the probability that people will say everything that needs to be said. We also realize that not all groups find working together smooth or easy. Those who eventually experience that the task is bigger than their own immediate needs, live with this tension and participate constructively. The tension that we live with as facilitators is that our design does not include explicit methods for uncovering and fixing such situations. This is a philosophic choice on our part – to put the burden on small groups, on the theory that we soon will be gone, and they will still have their issues.

Contracting for Success

An unspoken request to consultants goes something like this: "Give us methods, advice, data so powerful that you will take away ambiguity and allow us to bounce back and forth between contentment and renewal without ever having to visit confusion or chaos. Meet all our individual and collective needs." Consultants who accept that contract inevitably fail. It is not given to us to do for others what they only can do for themselves. (The commonly observed disappointment

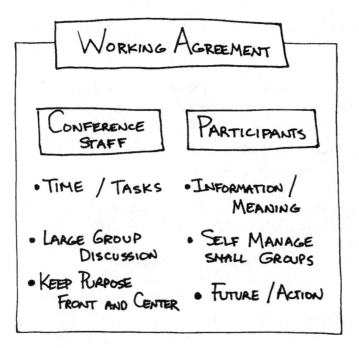

with "flavors of the month" and "quick fixes" results from the repetition of a fantasy – that *this* method will exempt us from having to muddle through for ourselves. Or put another way, if the consultant assumes leadership, we're off the hook.)

We believe the spirit of our deal in a future search is that we manage task assignments, large group dialogues and dynamics, and the consideration of unforeseen glitches if they affect the task. Participants manage everything else. If we take a more intrusive role than this, we are more likely to keep important things from happening. People discovering the joys and paradoxes of taking charge of themselves, for example. Participants have thanked us for staying out of the way and letting them work. That's our payoff. We have learned, after years of experimentation, to do something that works!

Facilitator Guidelines – A Summary

VALUES

- Belief in peoples' ability to self-manage their work.
- Desire to create open systems.
- Commitment to democracy in action.

SKILLS NEEDED

- Managing large group dynamics.
- Letting people struggle. Living with the unfamiliar.
- Planning *with* a group that includes skeptics.
- Trusting people to self-manage tasks without prior training.
- Stopping action if people fight or flee.
- Using designs faithful to key concepts/values.
- Saying "no" to conference requests that defeat the sponsor's purpose.
- Working on your own issues around "looking good," control, stereotyping, rescuing, lecturing, etc.

HOW TO SHARPEN SKILLS

- Attend future search conferences and/or SearchNet public workshops.
- Co-manage one or more future searches. Conferences benefit from two facilitators. Find a mentor.
- Read everything you can get your hands on.
- Talk with experienced conference facilitators and participants.
- Join self-development activities – skill-building and personal growth groups.

ADVICE FOR FACILITATORS

Develop your own capabilities. Our design "works." And so do others. We're also confident that all designs fail because the magic is not in the markers. For "it" to work, *we* have to work — on ourselves. To accept polarities in groups, we start by accepting them in ourselves. To allow others on the roller coaster, we need to know what it's like to ride it ourselves. Sometimes we have too little experience to do what we want and sometimes we run into problems we can't control.

So our advice is to do what excites you, not what excites us; consult your own experience and style. Pay attention to what you think, feel, and say as you manage a conference. We strongly urge you to work with a partner, preferably somebody different from you. Large groups take a lot of psychic and physical energy. There's too much going on for one person to manage it all. Together we do things neither could do alone. When one of us works, the other can relax — a little.

Our way of working is a unique amalgam of our lives, the way we think, our commitments, our training, and our limitations, all of which determines both our design and what comes out of our mouths at any moment. We suit some people, but we're not everybody's answer. We work both from intuition and a belief in the power of structures and processes over content. In that sense ours is not a "how-to-do-it" book but rather how-we-do-us in a future search. If you resonate to our concepts and practices, you probably can use them in ways that suit you.

CHAPTER 10

After the Conference

"Action groups formed at the end of the
conference are working on plans and ideas
in housing, economic development, diver-
sity, and fund raising...these groups have
been joined by dozens of new faces – people
who weren't at the March conference but
heard about its activities through other
people or this newsletter.

– Santa Cruz County *Future Search News*

> "I've been through
> a lot of these and
> you walk out feeling
> warm and fuzzy.
> Here we walked out
> with a common set
> of goals, a plan and
> some ideas for
> action. We weren't
> going to go home
> and forget about
> this. There were
> definite assign-
> ments."

WHAT HAPPENS AFTER A FUTURE SEARCH? That de-
pends largely on what people sign up to do. No sign
ups, no action. The fact is nobody knows how to get
other people to do things they don't want to do.

Traditional change theory has it that we have to "build in"
follow-up mechanisms. Future search theory holds that we
get more implementation when we attend to each stage of the
process, giving people ample opportunity to engage each
other. From many years of future searches, we know that
people are likely to carry out projects that matter to them if
they have enough support. They will create whatever struc-
tures they need. The only mechanism we need to "build in"
is the opportunity for people to sign up and get together.

There is always a temptation to shorten dynamic aspects
of a conference and "make more time for action planning."
We strongly believe in more time for action planning. But not

at the expense of the dynamic roller-coaster ride. To fall into that trap is to revert to a mode that has disappointed people repeatedly. If we short circuit the shared encounter we deprive the group of an experience that builds commitment.

A future search makes a big ripple in the life of an organization or community and the effects are felt for a long time. People invariably create projects and structures that take on a life of their own. These are not consultant-driven, nor do they require a lot of outside help to keep going. As a result we have a growing inventory of practices that keep the momentum over time. We have no prescriptions. Instead, we pay attention to what folks actually do.

Follow-Up Strategies

"At last I saw that everyone was getting together and saying, 'I'm going to do this. And whoever else wants to do it, come here."

Here's a review of what some conferences have actually done afterwards to act on common ground: *

- The Alliance for Employee Growth and Development began rotating quarterly meetings among different regions, so that people in every part of the country could participate in planning.

- ACM Siggraph, a trade association interest group, scheduled a public accountability meeting at the annual conference three months after the future search. Seven task forces reported on what was done and not done. They also set up on-line bulletin boards so that all members could participate in task force work via Internet.

- Bay State Skills Corporation, co-sponsor of Manufacturing and Massachusetts 2002, set up meetings with state legislators to brief them on outcomes and convened a proposal-writing committee that used the conference

*The authors want to thank Nancy Aronson, Tammy Blossom, John Hoopes, Drew Howick, Gail Ledesema, Christy McGraw, Susan Olson, Paul Pelkola, Joan Saries, Bill Schmidt and John VanDeusen for follow-up examples from conferences they have sponsored or run.

output to raise millions of dollars for a state-wide manufacturing extension service. Conference participants continue on advisory boards for the new service.

- Haworth, Inc., the office furniture manufacturer, made a 7-minute video, added a discussion guide, and made both available to all departments. In addition, task forces formed at the conference invited many other people to join their work, stimulating work redesign and quality improvement projects throughout the corporation.

- The Greater Santa Cruz Community Foundation formed a coordinating committee from conference planners and volunteers at the conference. They took on the job of publishing a regular newsletter, linking action groups, and providing meeting space, secretarial help, and other resources. A revolving rental loan fund was created for farm worker housing, other new housing projects were initiated, and task forces continued working on a cross-section of community visions. Several more future searches were planned.

- 3 M Corporation's internal consultants provided space for stakeholders to meet and continue planning, and the director of the sponsoring department set up a review meeting four months later. Output from the future search became input to the redesign of two divisions that had been involved in the conference.

- Kansas City Consensus initiated a series of additional future searches in many sectors – some run by facilitators trained in the initial implementation conference – with area schools districts and a "youth summit" for children age 13 and older. In regular review meetings ten action teams updated the community on progress in creating audio tours for visitors from other neighborhoods, a youth empowerment project to involve young people in decisions, and the use of schools as community centers.

"As a follow-up, we've been meeting and talking about strategies for housing that are not pie-in-the-sky. It's very pragmatic, more practical, doable kinds of things."

- Oak Hill Elementary School created a giant grid with action teams across the top and time frames down the side. As groups reported their plans in a follow-up meeting, they were posted on the grid. The whole meeting got involved in prioritizing the efforts. The grid stayed visible, and was updated regularly as action teams continued to meet for follow-up.

- Sun Prairie, WI school district recruited six local residents as facilitators to help advisory teams after the future search. Through newspaper ads and direct mail local residents were recruited to join the teams. Each team had a cross-section of stakeholders – board, administration, students, government officials, business people, teachers, and labor union members. About half the volunteers came from the conference and half from the community. They met twice as a total group with the Board of Education to report progress. A stakeholders' steering team coordinated for a year after the conference.

- A Federal Bankruptcy Court discovered that many people were excited and they wanted to get to work the moment the conference ended. However, they had not anticipated this development, and, to their dismay, nobody had meeting time available the week after the conference. They couldn't meet for several weeks and this slowed down the momentum. Moral: Keep calendars open after the conference if you want fast action.

- Mission College in Santa Clara, CA, found a great many non-participants eager to hear about the conference and to join in follow-up. However, so much else was going on they couldn't get anything out publicly for several months. Later, they realized that they should have produced a public report in the week following the conference, showing who participated, what was decided, and who to contact to become involved. Despite this glitch, faculty future search members, after a lead-

ership change later in the year, used the output in setting new directions.

- A Silicon Valley manufacturing conference formed a Manufacturing Education Council with several Silicon Valley firms and colleges that had attended the conference. They brought in numerous others, who began working on a Bay Area service center for manufacturing – one of 100 planned for the United States. Business, university, and state government officials who had met in the conference became an ongoing advocacy and action group. Another task force, meeting on its own time, got a grant to develop a manufacturing core curriculum for 107 California community colleges.

- Members of a homeless veterans organization had so much on their plate they couldn't imagine forming new groups or taking on more work. Instead, they decided to expand what they already had in place, shaping existing projects based on what had come out of the future search. People were greatly relieved to find they did not have to add new responsibilities.

- Forté Systems, a software service firm, put their mind map and other charts on an office wall, created a "buddy" system with people who did not attend the conference, and held an open house for all employees and family members to present their future plans, strategies, and new ideas for involving people.

Chapter 10

AFTER THE CONFERENCE

"I was gang member. I went through a lot. Most of the time, when they said, 'Let's do this for the youth,' then they'd say, 'Where's the money at?' In this conference they didn't even mention money. They just said we're going to do it."

Sponsor Tip

From these and other cases we see a clear advantage to having periodic review meetings that bring together stakeholders from the original conference and other interested parties. People report what they are doing, what they have planned, and how other people can sign up to help. A chance to do further action-planning can be built in. A review meeting requires no more than four to six hours and usually

starts with task force or individual action reports, for example:

- What we said we were going to do;
- What we have done;
- What we're going to do next; and

- What help we need.

A design that works well goes like this:

- Invited groups (newcomers sit in appropriate groups) have half an hour to prepare 5 minute presentations, based on items above (30 minutes)
- Groups present and discuss their reports (45 minutes)
- Groups do further work as indicated by the content of their report outs (One to two hours)
- Summary reports of second round, next steps (30 minutes)

Some organizations have followed this pattern for a year or more. It is a simple, inexpensive way to keep action planning fresh, connected, and relevant for all parties.

Consultant Tip

If you've done your job, *you're* done. Of course, you can contract for further services. However, when people take responsibility for their own planning, they implement their plans with or without consulting help, as the examples above indicate. Often a coordinating committee is formed at the end of the conference; volunteers join steering committee members who want to stay involved. The committee links action groups, keeps communication flowing, and accepts responsibility for distributing the documentation.

The examples here tell us that these conferences open up new ways of imagining constructive change processes. They are less dependent on consultants, more congruent with what self-motivated human beings are actually capable of doing. They offer clues to how we might parlay our separate efforts without burdening ourselves with expensive, complicated, and exhausting "total systems change strategies." Changing large organizations, cultures, communities, or whole societies is something we only know how to talk about. Running a 16+ hour future search conference is something we can learn how to do. Hundreds of SearchNet members have done that. We invite readers of this book to join us.

ABOUT SEARCHNET

SearchNet has three purposes. One is to help people master the basic principles of future search conferences. A second is to provide a match-making service — between community-based non-profits that need planning help and consultants who want to serve. The third is to provide information, tools, and services that will help our members to help themselves.

We are a grassroots movement. We exist only because so many folks want to learn future search planning methods by helping their communities. As individuals we're making ripples. Together we can make waves. If each of us runs one conference a year, we stimulate common futures and new action plans among thousands of people. As we widen the discovery of common ground among people we need and have not met, or people we distrust and have stereotyped, we enable creative action on many issues.

To belong, you don't have to be a consultant. Anybody can join if they will do one pro-bono SearchNet activity a year in the non-profit world — run, organize, or sponsor a conference, provide facilities to people sponsoring conferences, mentor or "shadow" consult to facilitators, provide scholarships to people who want to learn, research the process, share your learning, and so on. We provide progress reports in SearchNEWS, a benefit of membership. We intend to keep SearchNet simple, inexpensive, locally-based, and interactive. We hope to show that if each of us does locally what we care about we can make a difference to the future of our planet. We welcome your ideas, projects, and partnership.

SearchNet Information: 1-800-951-6333

Logistics

Conference Sites, Room Set-Up, and Materials

> "Rooms without a view are prisons for the people who have to stay in them....When people are in a place for any length of time, they need to be able to refresh themselves by looking at a world different from the one they are in, and with enough of its own variety and life to provide refreshment."
>
> – Christopher Alexander

EXPERIENCED FACILITATORS HAVE LEARNED, mostly by trial and error, how the quality of a conference setting influences the well-being of people engaged in future search. We have drawn upon the expertise of Robert Weisbord, an architect interested in holistic health, who has attended many conferences and written a guide for SearchNet members. He based his recommendations in part on Christopher Alexander's studies of how people have used space over many centuries in diverse cultures.

Future Search Room Requirements

The future search conference room and surrounding setting are variables we can control. So we always stack the deck for success by holding our meeting in a place where people want to be. It sounds simpler than it is. Many hotel and resort

conference centers are well-designed for the latest audiovisual hardware, software, techno-hookups, and night time entertainment – but they have forgotten the windows. People interact more successfully in spaces where they feel good. We can always find wall space in windowless hotel "dungeon" rooms, but our requirements for rooms with wall space and windows have driven many a conference logistics person crazy.

In 1993, we found a "technology" that enabled breakthroughs in design, set-up, and room requirement. These are Foamcore boards, 4 feet x 8 feet x 3/16" or 1/4" per sheet. They are very light and can be taped together. They are stiff enough to stand against existing walls or pillars and they are light enough to be placed sideways on easel ledges (two easels hold one board).

We discovered that Foamcore boards on easels also make good room dividers for rooms that are too big. We now send 12 sheets to every conference if we don't have adequate blank walls. We use six boards for the time lines, three for the mind map, and three for the common futures activity. We also encourage conference centers to stock these boards, as they do easels, so that we don't have to ship them around.

In Search of an Ideal Conference Room

"If you can find a room that feels good to be in," says Robert Weisbord, "chances are you've got a good future search room." Below are some rules of thumb that increase the chances a room will feel good. The closer we come to these ideal conditions, the more creative our conferences are, and the happier we and the participants are doing the work.

• *The Right Shape and Size.* Rooms that are square to square/rectangular work best. We look for rooms where the length is less than two times the width. A room that is 40 feet wide by 50 feet long is a wonderful space for 64 people arranged at eight tables of eight each. People can communicate across the room and still feel connected. In a much larger or more rectangular room, we lose this critical intimacy.

• *Windows.* Natural light, outside air, and a refreshing view of the world beyond the room are the great benefits of windows. Ideal rooms have windows that open on at least two sides, reminding us there is a world outside. Our senses stay more alive in natural light and with the occasional smell of outside air. At the Marconi Conference Center in Marshall California, for example, participants can glimpse Tomales Bay in the distance and smell the flowers and trees through the open windows. At Mohonk Mountain House in New Paltz, NY, they catch the majesty of the surrounding mountains and the serene beauty of a glacial lake. Urban sights, sounds, and smells can be equally as stimulating and inspirational. Another bonus is that day light means we use less electricity and are less exposed to the depressing effects of artificial light, which is rarely full-spectrum.

• *Wall Space.* We need wall and/or Foamcore board space for the time lines and mind map. More, since we want all information on flip charts to be in full view throughout, we need a lot of wall space. We need space for our Common Future and Potential Projects summaries. We also need wall space for hanging the newspaper articles if folks bring them, and for an (optional) picture gallery.

• *Round Tables.* We prefer round tables over rectangular tables. Round tables serve the future search process because they foster a non-hierarchical space for good interaction between participants. We request five foot rounds for groups of eight or nine. Once we were faced with tables that were too big in a room that was too small (we hadn't heeded our own warning to visit the search site beforehand). Our crisis ended when we found a bigger room in which the tables worked, but we had been ready to go with eight chairs in a circle, foregoing the tables altogether if need be.

• *Comfortable Chairs.* Participants spend much of each day sitting, and a great deal of they time turning their attention back and forth between the entire room and others at their table. Chairs that have arms and can swivel and roll work best.

Room Set-Up

The set-up takes us about two hours. We get a lot of help from volunteers on our steering commitee.

FINISHED-ROOM CHECK LIST – A GENERIC DESCRIPTION

- Each **table** is set with:
 - Table number in middle
 - 1 box of magic markers
 - 1 roll of masking tape
- Three **time lines** are on the walls, the central one on Foamcore, the others wherever we can find wall space.
- The **mind map paper** is on the wall or mounted on Foamcore. A circle is drawn with the future search topic in the middle.
- The six opening **flip chart**s are made and posted:
 - Welcome
 - Open Systems Chart
 - Agenda
 - 4 room apartment
 - Working Agreement
 - Groundrules
- Flip chart **easels** for each table are leaning against the walls. (Because the group doesn't use them right away, we leave them folded – we appreciate the unobstructed view for the brief time that we have it.)
- The **future scenario supplies** are laid out on another rectangular table against the wall.
- **Sound System**. Regardless of the size of the room, an amplification system is often a good idea. If acoustics turn out to be perfect when the room is full, you can always put the system aside. Three microphones – one for the facilitators and one for each side of the room works well. Music is nice during breaks.
- **Registration Table** with participants' workbooks, badges, logistics information, etc. Each participant's workbook contains the schedule, a participant list, mixed and stakeholder table assignments, worksheets for each task, handouts, note paper, etc. Conference planners have used ring binders, spiral bound books, and folders with sheets placed in pockets.

Resource
Table

Conference Focus (Time Line 2' x 24')

1960's ——————> 1970's ——————> 1980's

Personal (Time Line 2' x 24')

1960's ——————> 1970's ——————> 1980's

Eight stakeholders per table

1960's ————> 1970's ————> 1980's

Global (Time Line 2' x 24')

(Not to scale)

Mind Map (12' x 6')

Hanging the Time Lines

If we don't have the wall space for the time lines, we use six Foamcore sheets taped together standing upright to make an 8 foot high by 24 foot long wall. *Hint* – if you tape them together accordion fashion (like a dressing room screen, with tape on alternating sides) they can be folded, stored, shipped, and reused. We have also used three Foamcore sheets placed side-ways on easels to make a "time line wall" that is 4 feet high and 24 feet long.

To create the time lines, we cut three sheets of butcher paper 2 feet high and 24 feet long. We hang one 24 foot strip across the middle of our "time line wall" – making it easy for people to write on it. We label the time line in the middle with the name of our conference focus and date it across the top with the beginning and end of each era indicated. We cut and date two identical 2 foot x 24 foot strips, one for Global and one for Personal data. Since we generally review the past over three eras, we have an 8 foot span for each era. We want the dates to match when the time lines are assembled in parallel for the analysis.

We hang the two time lines – Global and Personal – in separate sections of the room so that groups of people have easy access for writing. We don't need continuous wall space for the Global and Personal time lines. We can divide them into three 8 foot sections or two 12 foot sections. We just want to mark the sections clearly so that we can easily match them up for our review of the past.

The groups that are assigned the Global and Personal time line reports, will move the data bases and align them with the conference task time line on the (Foamcore) time line wall. Global goes above and Personal below.

Hanging the Mind Map

If we don't have adequate wall space, we use three Foamcore sheets taped together, standing upright to make a wall 8 feet high x 12 feet long. On this wall we center a butcher paper rectangle approximately 6 feet high x 12 feet long. We have also used two Foamcore sheets placed side by side, resting on easel ledges, making a mind map wall 4 feet x 16 feet. It worked well. We draw a circle in the center of the paper and write in the name of the conference focus – the organization, the community, or the issue.

To Sum Up. . .

The perfect room for eight tables of eight people each is 2000 square feet, 50 feet x 40 feet. It has large windows on two sides with flat walls on the other two sides. It has good lighting, temperature control, and acoustics. We want enough room for people to move around comfortably (obvious) and with windows that let in outside light (not so obvious). Our workspace, plus comfortable chairs and healthy food, are among the few aspects of a conference we can control. So we do everything possible to control them.

FUTURE SEARCH CONFERENCE MATERIALS CHECKLIST

For Partipants
- Participant Invitation letter - see sample in Resource Section.
- Administrative assistance at Conference registration.
- Name Badges.

For Participant Workbooks
- Participant workbook binders.
- Conference participant list.
- Table assignments for mixed groups and stakeholder groups.

For Room Set-up
- Table numbers.
- 12 Foamcore boards, 4 ' x 8' by 3/16" or 1/4" thick.
- One box of water soluble magic markers for each table and two boxes for the facilitators. (We like broad tip Mr. Sketch.)
- One flip chart easel with full flip chart pads for each table and two for facilitators.
- Butcher paper: three strips, 2' wide x 24' long for the time lines, two strips 4' wide x 12' long for the mind map.
- One roll of masking tape for each table and one for facilitators.
- Colored dots (3/8 or 1/2 inch): a different color for each stakeholder group, seven dots per person.
- Supplies for future scenarios — enough for each mixed group: construction paper, scissors, scotch tape, glitter, glue, pipe cleaners, stickers, and anything else you can imagine.
- Amplification system: one microphone for facilitators and two for group — one for each side of the room.
- Round tables for small groups.
- One small table for facilitators, Two rectangular tables — one for mementos and one for scenario supplies.

APPENDIX B

Sample Workbook

There's no such thing as a typical workbook. We supply a set of worksheets modified to reflect the specific conference. We have found these useful in helping people track the tasks, and they are easily modified or skipped entirely if developments require it. The "handouts" are generic items summarizing some of our thoughts about the process. Conference sponsors often add table assignments, a name and address list of participants, housekeeping information about the meeting site, and other information they want people to have.

The worksheets help people track through the conference tasks. We adapt them to each situation, changing the language if need be. The time frames grow out of planning, along with the purpose of the conference.

"OUR TOWN" 2005

Working Together to Build Our Future
FUTURE SEARCH CONFERENCE AGENDA
Conference Staff: Marv Weisbord and Sandra Janoff

MONDAY, JUNE 5, 1995

1:00 pm – 6:00 pm OPENING AND WELCOME

CONFERENCE OVERVIEW & PROCEDURES

FOCUS ON THE PAST:
Highlights and Milestones
Goal: Appreciate our history, trends we
have experienced, what the past means to us

FOCUS ON THE PRESENT: Current Trends
Goal: Understand the forces having an
impact on "Our Town" now

TUESDAY, JUNE 6, 1995

8:30 am – 12:30 pm FOCUS ON THE PRESENT (continued)

12:30 pm – 1:30 pm LUNCH**"Our Town" Future Search Conference**

1:30 pm – 5:30pm FOCUS ON THE FUTURE
Goal: Imagine an ideal future for "Our Town"

WEDNESDAY, JUNE 7, 1995

8:30 am – 1:00 pm COMMON GROUND ON THE FUTURE
Goal: Discover our common future and
direction

PLANNING FOR THE FUTURE
Goal: Make short and long-term action plans

1:00 pm NEXT STEPS AND CLOSING

NOTE: All sessions will begin and end on time. There will be
breaks each morning and afternoon, with refreshments

FRAMEWORK FOR A FUTURE SEARCH CONFERENCE

How this conference differs from typical participative meetings:

• The **WHOLE SYSTEM** participates – a cross-section of as many interested parties as practical. That means more diversity and less hierarchy than is usual in a working meeting, and a chance for each person to be heard and to learn other ways of looking at the task at hand.

• Future scenarios – for an organization, community or issue – are put into **HISTORICAL** and **GLOBAL** perspective. That means thinking globally together before acting locally. This feature enhances shared understanding and greater commitment to act. It also increases range of potential actions.

• People **SELF-MANAGE** their work, and use **DIALOGUE** – not "problem- solving" as the main tool. That means helping each other do the tasks and taking responsibility for our perceptions and actions.

• **COMMON GROUND** rather than "conflict management," is the frame of reference. That means honoring our differences rather than having to reconcile them.

"Our Town" / Handout 1

WORKING AGREEMENT

Conference staff: Sandra Janoff and Marv Weisbord

Conference Staff	Participants
• Set Time and Tasks	• Provide information/Make meaning
• Large Group Discussions	• Manage own small groups
• Keep Purpose Front and Center	• Future scenarios/Action steps

GROUND RULES

- • All ideas are valid
- • Everything is written on flip charts
- • Listen to Each Other
- • Observe time frames
- • Seek common ground and action
- • Differences and problems are acknowledged – not "worked"

"Our Town" / Handout 2

SELF-MANAGEMENT LEADERSHIP ROLES

Each small group manages its own discussion, data, time, and reports. Here are useful roles for self-managing this work. **Leadership roles can be rotated.** Divide up the work as you wish:

- **DISCUSSION LEADER** – Assures that each person who wants to speak is heard within time available. Keeps group on track to finish on time.

- **TIMEKEEPER** – Keeps group aware of time left. Monitors report-outs and signals time remaining to person talking.

- **RECORDER** – Writes group's output on flip charts, using speaker's words. Asks people to restate long ideas briefly.

- **REPORTER** – Delivers report to large group in time allotted.

FOCUS ON THE PAST

Purpose: Develop a community picture of our world, values, and histories.

1. Alone, make notes on memorable **personal, global, and local** events that represent to you notable milestones and/or turning points.
2. Use a magic marker to transfer your notes to time lines on the wall.

PERSONAL
What You Did? (Why Important?)

1960's _____

1970's _____

1980's to Now _____

"Our Town" / Worksheet 1

GLOBAL EVENTS
What Happened? (Why Important?)

1960's _____

1970's _____

1980's to now _____

"Our Town" / Worksheet 2

184

LOCAL COMMUNITY, ORGANIZATION OR ISSUE
What Happened (Why Important)

1960's _____

1970's _____

1980's to Now _____

"Our Town" / Worksheet 3

FOCUS ON THE PAST
"The past is prelude..."

REPORTS ARE DUE AT_____O'CLOCK

Purposes: Identify themes and patterns that have shaped our community. Establish a context for our shared future.

- Self-manage: Decide on leadership roles for your group.
- Each table views our histories from a different perspective.
- Discuss the time lines and write your summary on flip charts.
- Prepare a **3-minute** summary report.

TABLE ASSIGNMENTS

1. Table(s)_____
a. Looking at the **Personal** time line, what story can you tell about us—the folks in this room?
b. Scan the other timelines. What connections do you see?

2. Table(s)_____
a. Looking at the **Global** time line, what story can you tell about our recent history?
b. Scan the other timelines. What connections do you see?

3. Table(s)_____
a. Looking at the **Local** time line, what story can you tell about our recent history?
b. Scan the other timelines. What connections do you see?

Notes...

"Our Town" / Worksheet 4

FOCUS ON THE PRESENT

Trends Affecting Our Future

Purpose: Build a shared context of our concerns and priorities.

(This task has two parts.)

Article Summary: Go around the table. Each person summarizes article they brought and why it is important to our future. (2 minutes per person.)

Notes (for your own use):

Group Mind Map: The total group will create a "mind map" of all trends affecting us right now.

Ground rules for mind-mapping:

1. This is a group brainstorm — no evaluation, no censorship.
2. Person who names the issue says where it goes on the map.
3. Give examples. Speak in terms of WHO and/or WHAT. ("More cellular telephones" is an example of the trend toward "better communications.")

"Our Town" / Worksheet 5

FOCUS ON THE PRESENT

Stakeholder Perspectives On External Trends

REPORTS ARE DUE AT_____O'CLOCK

Purpose: Assess our present global situation in relation to our task.

Self-manage: Decide on leadership roles for your group

1. Talk over TRENDS of concern to YOUR STAKE-HOLDER group. Make your own map on a flip chart showing how these trends are related and how they affect you. On the map, note examples of what **you** are DOING RIGHT NOW in response to these trends. Also note what **you** WANT TO DO that you aren't doing right now.

2. Prepare a 4-Minute report.

"Our Town" / Worksheet 6

FOCUS ON THE PRESENT

"Prouds" and "Sorries"- Owning Up

REPORTS ARE DUE AT_____O'CLOCK

Purpose: Assess PRESENT (current reality) in our relationship to our future and to other stakeholders. [NOTE—This is an experience in owning up to what is, not blaming or problem-solving. The motto is, "Own it, don't moan it!"]

Self-manage: Decide on leadership roles for your group

1. List what YOU are doing RIGHT NOW that you are PROUD of in YOUR RELATIONSHIP to our task. List things YOU are doing RIGHT NOW that you are SORRY about.

2. Select your "PROUDEST PROUDS" and "SORRIEST SORRIES."

3. Reporters: Prepare a 3-minute report.

Notes...

"Our Town" / Worksheet 7

FOCUS ON THE FUTURE
Ideal Future Scenario

PRESENTATIONS ARE DUE AT _____ O'CLOCK.

Purpose: To imagine a future you want to work toward.

1. Put yourself _____ years into the future.
 Visualize the community you *really* want as if it
 exists now. What is life like?
2. List your **accomplishments** since 1995, with
 special reference to:

(NOTE: The list below can be generated by a steering committee or the whole
conference just before starting the task.)

—Nature of community leadership
—Mix of population
—Types and location of housing
—Zoning and planning policy
—Financing methods for new and existing housing
—Employment opportunities
—Relations between county and university
—Community services and facilities
—Transportation
—Relations between north and south county areas
—Public policies, community initiatives
—Other highly-desirable features

Spend enough time to imagine concretely the world in which your
group wants to live. This is an exercise in creative dreaming – of
the kind of community you want to work toward..

3. On a flip chart, brainstorm the major **barriers** that
 you had to overcome, and the **opportunities** you
 worked with.
4. Choose a **creative** way to present your vision as if it
 is happening now.

Examples: • A TV Special • Magazine Cover Story • Drama
• A Day in the Life • A Work of Art • Other – your choice.

"Our Town" / Worksheet 8

COMMON GROUND ON THE FUTURE

-Notes-

Purpose: To discover the common ground desired by the conference.

1. Note desired themes – **what we want** – that are being presented in the scenarios. This is our potential common ground agenda.

2. Collect examples, projects, ideas that groups use as ways to get there – **how we may do it.**

COMMON THEMES – (WHAT) _____

PROJECTS, IDEAS, EXAMPLES – (HOW) _____

"Our Town" / Worksheet 9

COMMON GROUND FOR THE FUTURE

Purpose: To confirm the common future desired by the whole conference.

1. Prepare a list of themes that make up our (1) **common future agenda (what)** and a second list of (2) **examples of ways to work toward it (how).**

2. Make a third list of **unresolved differences (not agreed here).**

3. As a whole conference, we will merge the lists into one. We will compare the lists and talk about on what they mean to us. **Examples** are only that. We do not need to agree on them.

Note: We will acknowledge and seek to understand what we *really* want together. We will accept and hear, but not reconcile, differences if they arise. People can and should continue to work toward their preferred goals, whether or not supported by the whole conference. Our purpose **here** is to base our **joint** action planning on common futures, making implementation more certain.

Notes....

"Our Town" / Worksheet 10

PERSONAL ACTION PLANNING

(This sheet is for your own use.)

Purpose: To brainstorm short and long term action steps. What are steps you want to take RIGHT NOW to work toward our common future agenda?

Short term actions (next 3 months)

WHAT	HELP NEEDED FROM	DUE DATE

Long term actions (next 3 years)

WHAT	HELP NEEDED FROM	DUE DATE

"Our Town" / Worksheet 11

STAKEHOLDER [or VOLUNTARY GROUP] ACTION PLANNING

(This sheet is to record group planning ideas and decisions)

YOUR STAKEHOLDER OR TASK GROUP_____

REPORTS ARE DUE AT_____O'CLOCK

Purpose: To decide on short and long term action steps. What are steps you will take as a group to work toward our common future agenda?

Short term actions (next 3 months)

WHAT	HELP NEEDED FROM	DUE DATE

Long term actions (next 3 years)

WHAT	HELP NEEDED FROM	DUE DATE

"Our Town" / Worksheet 12

A Future Search Design Guide

March 1995

We use this framework in designing our conferences. The general pattern is to do three kinds of work for each exploration. First, everybody generates an information base. Second, small groups decide what it means to them. Third, small groups present to the whole, and the whole conference dialogues on the implications. Our rough norm is 45 minutes for each kind of work.

DAY 1

1:00 pm – 2:00 pm *Participants sit in Mixed Groups*
Welcome by sponsor
 and conference staff
Overview, agenda, dynamics,
 groundrules, etc.
Small group introductions

2:00 pm – 6:00 pm **REVIEWING THE PAST**
Worksheets 1 to 4
Reports and Discussion

Reorganize into Stakeholder Groups

PRESENT TRENDS (External)
Worksheet 5
Small groups discuss trends
Group builds Mind Map
Individuals identify concerns
 with dots

DAY 2

8:30 am – 12:30 pm Participants meet at
 the mind map wall
Whole group discusses
 major clusters and themes

PRESENT TRENDS, cont.
Worksheet 6
Reports and discussion

OWNING THE PRESENT
Worksheet 7
Reports and discussion

Reorganize into Mixed Groups

12:30 pm – 3:00pm CREATE IDEAL FUTURES
(Includes lunch)
Worksheet 8

3:00 pm – 4:30 pm PRESENT FUTURE SCENARIOS
During presentations
Worksheet 9

4:30 pm – end COMMON GROUND ON THE FUTURE
Worksheet 10

DAY 3

8:30 am – 1:00 pm Whole group meets at wall
REALITY DIALOGUE

*Reorganize into stakeholder
or voluntary groups*

ACTION PLANNING
Usually two rounds of planning,
public reports, and discussing
commitments
Worksheets 11 and 12

Close

If more planning time is desired, we break at
noon for lunch and continue action planning
from 1:00 to 3:00 pm. This decision is made in
advance by the steering committee.

Sample Invitation Letter

Florida Atlantic University
College of Nursing

Dear_____

As a stakeholder in the future, you are cordially invited to participate as a member of the conference, Discovering Common Ground: The Future of Health. Healing & Environment, Lantana, Florida, February 23-25, 1995. You have been selected because of specific strengths and insights you can bring to the future search process.

The group of 48 participants (stakeholders) will convene at 11:00 am on Thursday, February 23 for registration and lunch, followed by a full afternoon session. We will conclude the conference with lunch, scheduled for 1:00 pm, on Saturday, February 25th. A detailed Agenda for the three days will be available at registration. We will be in residence at the Cenacle, a beautiful retreat setting on the intracoastal waterway.

The goal of the conference is to discover our common ground for the future of health, healing and the environment. Work of the conference is based on the assumption that the future doesn't just happen. The future results in part from what we do, or don't do, today. Through this conference, we will determine what the most desirable future of health, healing and the environment looks like to a cross section of key individuals, so that all of us can shape our present and future actions accordingly.

Working together in several small groups, as well as in the total group, we will pool information, analyze it and present conclusions. Before we bring the conference to closure, members of each key group (as listed below) will consider how these envisioned futures are likely to affect their own planning over the next five years. A report of the conference work will be made available to all participants to guide decision-making and planning.

Conference stakeholders have been chosen to represent the following key areas:
- Health
- Education
- Environment
- Business
- Public Service/Government
- Arts/Humanities/Religion/Healing

The conference will be guided by two consultants who are professionals in the fields of human behavior and large group dynamics; they are also experienced with and committed to the future search process. Their role in the conference

is to assist us to accomplish our tasks; they have no stake in the outcomes. The activities of the conference will be designed so that the conference belongs to each of us individually as well as to all of us collectively as does the future of health, healing and the environment.

Financing to support this conference has been solicited by the planning committee from local businesses and persons in the private sector. Therefore, there will be no cost to participants other than time, energy and a commitment to work with the future search process. While it is not an expectation, several invited individuals have volunteered a donation to the general fund. Please inquire if you want to be involved as a donor; we would welcome your gesture of support.

As part of the conference preparation, you are asked to bring with you for group sharing:

(1) An item or artifact that represents you as an individual;

(2) One or more current news stories, magazine articles or pictures that reflect, in your judgment, an event, trend or development that is shaping the future of health, healing and environment These articles could be related to education, social trends, geography, world politics, regional developments, changes in lifestyle, etc.—anything you believe should be taken into account in describing our future.

The members of the Steering Committee, welcome you to this very interesting venture. We look forward to an energizing and productive time together.

Sincerely,

Eleanor A Schuster
Conference Coordinator

Note: Our thanks to Eleanor Schuster and the Florida Atlantic University College of Nursing for permission to use this letter.

Selected Bibliography

Ackoff, Russell. *Redesigning the Future: The Systems Approach to Societal Problems. Wiley,* NY, 1974.

Agazarian, Yvonne M. & Sandra Janoff. "Systems Theory in Small Groups," in H. Kaplan and B. Sadock (eds.), *Comprehensive Textbook of Group Psychotherapy,* Williams & Wilkins, 1993.

Alban, Billie, & Barbara Bunker, co-editors. *Journal of Applied Behavioral Science,* Volume 28, No. 4, December 1992. Special Issue: "Large Group Interventions."

Alexander, Christopher. *A Pattern Language.* Oxford, New York, 1977.

Asch, Solomon. *Social Psychology,* Prentice-Hall, New York, 1952.

Berman, Morris. *Coming to Our Senses: Body and Spirit in the Hidden History of the West,* Bantam Books, New York, 1990.

Bertalanffy, Ludwig von. *General Systems Theory,* Wiley, New York, 1952.

Bion, Wilfred. *Experience in Groups*, Tavistock, London, 1961.

Buzan, Tony. *Use Both Sides of Your Brain*, Dutton, New York, 1976.

Emery, Fred E., & Eric L. Trist. "The Causal Texture of Organizational Environments." *Human Relations*, 1964, 18 (1), 21-32.

Emery, Fred E., & Eric L. Trist. *Toward a Social Ecology*, Plenum, New York, 1973.

Emery, Fred E. *The Emergence of a New Paradigm of Work.* Center for Continuing Education, Australian National University, Canberra, 1978.

Emery, Merrelyn, editor. *Participative Design for Participative Democracy*, Centre for Continuing Education, Australian National University, Canberra, Revised 1993.

Fritz, Robert. *The Path of Least Resistance*, Fawcett Columbine, New York, 1989.

Jacobs, Robert J. *Real Time Strategic Change.* Berrett-Koehler, San Francisco, 1994.

Janssen, C. *Personlig Dialektik.* (2nd ed.) Liber, Stockholm, 1982.

Jung, C.G. *Two Essays on Analytical Psychology*, translated by R.F.C. Hull, Princeton University Press, Princeton, NJ, 1966.

Korzybski, Alfred. *Science and Sanity.* 3rd Edition, International Non-Aristotelian Library, Institute of General Semantics, Lakeville, CT, 1948.

Lasch, Christopher. "The Revolt of the Elites," *Harper's Magazine*, November, 1994, pp. 39-49.

Lewin, Kurt. *Resolving Social Conflicts*, edited by Gertrude W. Lewin, Harper & Row, New York, 1948.

Lin Yun, Professor. Foreword to *Interior Design with Feng Shui*, by Sarah Rossbach, E.P. Dutton, New York, 1987.

Lippitt, Ronald. "Future Before You Plan." in *NTL Manager's Handbook.* Arlington, VA; NTL Institute, 1983.

Merrill, Alexandra. *Self-Differentiation: A Day with John and Joyce Weir* (Three Videotape Set). Blue Sky Productions, Philadelphia, 1991.

Naisbitt, John. *Megatrends: Ten New Directions Transfomring Our Lives.* Warner Books, New York, 1982.

Owen, Harrison. *Riding the Tiger: Doing Busines in a Transforming World.* Abbott Publishing, Potomoc, MD, 1991.

Schindler-Rainman, Eva, and Ronald Lippitt. *Building the Collaborative Community: Mobilizing Citizens for Action.* University of California, Irvine: 1980. Available from Energize, 215 438-8342.

Sheldrake, Rupert. *The Presence of the Past: Morphic Resonance and the habits of Nature. Vintage Books, New York, 1988.*

Weir, John. "Laboratory Method in Personal Growth," Chapter 13 in *Laboratory Method in Teaching and Learning,* by Lee Bradford, Kenneth Benne, Jack Gibb, and Ronald Lippitt, Science & Behavior Books, Palo Alto, 1971.

Weisbord, Marvin R. *Productive Workplaces: Organizing and Managing for Dignity, Meaning and Community,* Chapter 14, "Future Search." Jossey-Bass, San Francisco, 1987.

Weisbord, Marvin R. "How I Lied My Way Out of Latin and Became a Behavioral Scientist," *OD Practitioner,* a publication of the OD Network, Vol. 7, No. 2, July 1975.

Weisbord, Marvin R. and 35 Co-Authors, *Discovering Common Ground,* Berrett-Koehler, San Francisco, 1992.

Wheatley, Margaret J. *Leadership and the New Science.* Berrett-Koehler, San Francisco, 1992.

Wilber, Ken. *No Boundary: Eastern and Western Approaches to Personal Growth.* Shambhala, Boston & London, 1985.

SELECTED
BIBLIOGRAPHY

Index

About the Authors

Together Marvin Weisbord and Sandra Janoff, Ph.D., have 50+ years of professional group experience.

Marv practiced organizational consulting from 1969 to 1991 in factories, offices, colleges, medical schools, and hospitals. In the 1960's he was executive vice president of a family printing business that became one of the earliest self-managing team-based workplaces in the United States. He was a founder with Peter Block and Tony Petrella of the consulting firm Block Petrella Weisbord. For 20 years he was a member of NTL Institute for Applied Behavioral Science, where he ran learning laboratories in organizational diagnosis, team building, and consultation skills. He is an emeritus member of the European Institute for Transnational Studies, ran consulting workshops in Sweden and Norway in the 1970's and 1980's, and was a fellow at the Norwegian Institute of Technology in 1987.

Marv has been a regular guest lecturer in a Health Care Management Program at the University of Pennsylvania and in the Organization and Systems Renewal Program at Antioch University (Seattle). For six years he was an associate editor of *The Journal of Applied Behavioral Science*. He is the author of *Organizational Diagnosis* (1978) and *Productive Workplaces* (1987), used as texts in dozens of colleges and universities. He conceived and co-authored *Discovering Common Ground* (1992).

He stopped consulting in 1991 to devote his time to helping people learn and use future search processes in their own communities. He has been a board member of Resources for Human Development, parent organization of SearchNet, for 20 years. He leads an annual seminar "Men At Work" with John Weir and Michael Merrill. He is also an avid jazz pianist.

Sandra worked in public education from 1974 to 1984, teaching mathematics, physics and chemistry, and helping organize one of the first team-based high schools in the United States. She was involved in the design and implementation of open system methods through which students, teachers, parents, administrators, and school board members participated in curriculum development, planning, and operations. She also ran workshops in Pennsylvania schools on alternative practices in education.

From 1986 to 1990 she was a staff member in the Tavistock Conference sponsored by Temple University in Philadelphia and the Tavistock Working Conference sponsored by The Tavistock Institute of Human Relations in Oxford, England. Her research on relationships among organizational structure, behavior, and gender led to a doctoral dissertation, "The Influence of Legal Education on Moral Reasoning," published in the *Minnesota Law Review* and in *Feminist Jurisprudence: Taking Women Seriously – Cases and Materials*. In 1987 she, Marv, and Allan Kobernick co-founded Blue Sky Productions, a video company that has documented workplace innovations in many countries. As Blue Sky's CEO until 1992 she focused on product development, marketing, and strategic planning.

In 1991 she received a Ph.D. and was licensed as a clinical psychologist. In addition to consulting, she practices individual, couples, and group psychotherapy from a systems-centered theoretical base. She is a consulting affiliate with Friends Hospital where she runs training workshops in this methodology. She is co-author with Yvonne Agazarian of "Systems Thinking and Small Groups" for the *Comprehensive Textbook of Group Psychotherapy* (1993). She also does team building and staff development in organizations. Sandra has facilitated numerous future search conferences with Fortune 500's and small businesses, communities, and non-profit agencies, on issues such as manufacturing, housing, and education.

This book represents the fruits of Marv and Sandra's collaboration since 1987. Together they plan and lead conferences, coach facilitators, and offer a semi-annual public workshop, "Managing A Future Search." In 1993 they founded SearchNet, a non-profit network dedicated to community service, learning, and colleagueship among practitioners. They are partners in Future Search Associates, a consulting consortium committed to supporting community initiatives through their private sector efforts.